We Have a Child for You

Fostering
in
Rural Nova Scotia

Kathleen Foster-Alfred

We Have a Child for You
© 2023 Kathleen Foster-Alfred

Cover: Rebekah Wetmore
Editor: Andrew Wetmore

ISBN: 978-1-990187-78-0
First edition May, 2023

MOOSE HOUSE
PUBLICATIONS

2475 Perotte Road
Annapolis County, NS
B0S 1A0

moosehousepress.com
info@moosehousepress.com

We live and work in Mi'kma'ki, the ancestral and unceded territory of the Mi'kmaw People. This territory is covered by the "Treaties of Peace and Friendship" which Mi'kmaw and Wolastoqiyik (Maliseet) People first signed with the British Crown in 1725. The treaties did not deal with surrender of lands and resources but in fact recognized Mi'kmaq and Wolastoqiyik (Maliseet) title and established the rules for what was to be an ongoing relationship between nations. We are all Treaty people.

Dedication

This book is dedicated to a friend who motivated me to take action and make this book a reality. Melissa Myrick is a blunt, outspoken person who took away the permission I'd given myself to sit back, binge-watch TV series and play video games. She taught me that age and circumstance should not prevent me from having goals.

I couldn't argue with her logic and found myself casting about for a project that would occupy me with a positive activity. In my reflections, I realized that fostering was one of the most rewarding experiences of my life and I wanted so much to share what these wonderful children taught me.

I am so grateful to Melissa for rejecting my complacency and I only wish she had come into my life sooner.

The book, in and of itself, is a dedication to the children who crossed our threshold and to them I will always be grateful for sharing a part of their lives with our family.

The author has changed people's names and the details of events, and has combined the attributes of some people, to protect their privacy.

We Have a Child for You

Kathleen Foster-Alfred

1: We have a child for you

Often when people experience a significant event, they are able to recall minute details about what is happening around them at that moment in time. A clarity that freezes images, accentuates sounds and even exaggerates smells.

I had none of that on the day I answered this particular phone call. The caller had a flat response to my greeting—six simple words that would change our world forever.

"We have a child for you."

I felt time pause briefly and then I stepped towards the precipice. I was just a little confused.

"You do?" I constrained my surprise. I was totally off guard but desperately trying to sound calmly expectant. I had not anticipated hearing from Children's Aid—not now, not ever.

My husband, Wade, and I had applied to be foster parents well over a year earlier. We had been involved with some troubled teens, usually friends of my teenage daughter, but throughout my life there were episodes when other people's children ended up on my doorstep.

After applying to be foster parents, we completed

7

a course that brutally laid out some of the circumstances and situations we would be dealing with. It was more than an orientation and lasted several weeks of nighttime classes.

We benefited from instructions from social workers, medical professionals, current foster parents and so forth. So many kids coming from diverse backgrounds—our involvement promised to be interesting.

I have to say my husband was not enthusiastic after hearing some of the lectures on protective measures we would have to take for our own safety. On top of protocols Children's Aid recommended, we decided that we could never leave him in a room alone with any child. There was the issue of adult foster children coming forward later in life to make allegations and, although many are legitimate charges, some are pure nuisance cases designed to elicit money from innocent parents.

We decided my husband would guard himself from such possibilities by not being alone with any foster child, anytime, anywhere. Multiple children would be okay but there would always be a risk if we didn't strictly adhere to this rule. It would be cumbersome to enforce but absolutely mandatory for him.

We finished all the workshops and attended all the lectures, watching other couples drop out along the way. Some changed their minds after getting details about some of the situations they might encounter, but others were dropped for not quite having what it would take.

One couple confessed to me that the only reason they were there was to make money. They had fallen on hard times and decided taking in kids would buffer their shortfall without them really having to do anything at all. I mentally said goodbye to them and they disappeared shortly after.

We sat by the phone expectantly for months, and no word. We then moved out to the country and started a poultry farm.

It is odd that when we initially applied to foster, we were living in a town in a nice house with only one spare room. We would never have been able to take more than one child at a time. Then we moved out to the farm in a large country house with six bedrooms, with only myself, my husband, daughter Sarah and son Brent (part-time), so we had room to spare.

We hadn't heard a word from Children's Aid after all our training and assumed maybe we hadn't made the cut. I didn't see a problem with their strict background checks and references. The course we took had ended without any certification and we all had gone our own ways to wait for what might happen next. It was a shock to now hear from them out of the blue.

The social worker started to provide some details about the young teenager, but I had to interrupt. "This isn't a really good time." My sister had sent her four kids out to us for the month of August and, even though we had plenty of room, it could still get a little hectic.

"No, that's perfect," she said, and continued past my protests to describe a child who had had a troublesome history with a lot of counsellors and psychiatric involvement. "It will be great to be somewhere where there isn't a lot of focus on her."

As brief as the introduction was, I learned that Cynthia had been a bit of a tornado in her own home and was not co-operating with any efforts to work out her issues. She came from a small village where she had made life impossible for her parents, refusing to follow the most basic house rules, and, as will happen in a small place, had become involved with a bad crowd.

Her parents and social workers were aware that, somewhere along the road, Cynthia had been raped by the local drug dealer, but she refused to allow herself to be examined or to assist police in pursuing any charges. Apparently, the status of this guy and what he did had elevated him in the community and no one would dare to report any wrong-doing connected to him.

It was like an upside-down world. The more heinous his actions, the more he was presented as a hero.

As the social worker provided further details, my confidence that we could be that safe haven for the lost was beginning to fade. I had plenty of experience with kids and wasn't unfamiliar with those experiencing behavioural disorders, but Cynthia would be a test. This would be our first ward and we had to make it right.

I felt the children left in our care would be like fledgling birds, fallen from their nest. We weren't the parents but we would have to make sure we took the greatest care in how we handled something so delicate and fragile.

Cynthia's biological parents were still in the picture but, despite their best efforts, they had lost control. They were working with Children's Aid to resolve issues and bring their fractured family back together.

The agency didn't waste any time. They were going to bring Cynthia out that evening and we quickly prepared one of the rooms for her arrival. I filled the kids in on our visitor, leaving out the personal details, and everyone was excited to meet her and make her feel welcome.

My own daughter Maggie was 15 the same age as Cynthia. Suggestions were flying and Maggie thought it would be an advantage to have the two of them share a room. Children's Aid was clear in insisting each child have their own room. They needed privacy and a safe space to call their own.

It wasn't easy to get Maggie to dial it back. "She's not a puppy," I insisted.

It was a flurry of activity and I was happy to see them all so supportive of what we were doing.

This would be a major transition for Cynthia, as an only child coming from a small home. Our home was a farm with plenty of poultry—meat chickens, egg layers, turkeys, Muscovy ducks and guinea fowl.

11

There was the six-bedroom farmhouse, an old carriage shed, a long-abandoned dairy barn, poultry coops and a garage.

The property was in East Earltown, at least a half-hour drive outside the town of Truro. The house was down a dirt road and at the end of a long winding driveway.

Situated on a gentle slope, 120 acres that had once been home to a dairy herd were now only partially in use. The fields were used for hay but the pine and spruce trees were slowly closing in on the property. On clear days we could see the Northumberland Strait in the distance, even though it was six or seven miles away.

When we first moved to the farm, we were sure we had seen the last of most of our friends, thinking no one would make the trek out to see us, but we were wrong. Friends came often to visit, have dinner or just sit and absorb the surrounding landscape.

We had two front porches, left and right, separated by an entrance that split the wide stoop in half. Decorated with stained glass and tall windows on three sides, the house was deceptively formal. When you looked down at it from the top of the driveway, it was like looking at a mural.

I had some Adirondack furniture, painted the shade of green that develops on oxidized copper, on both porches, creating an inviting atmosphere. Ancient, abandoned farm equipment was slowly dissolving into the land and, as we were only renting the property, it was not our call to remove the relics.

Every year someone came and cut the hay, leaving big rolls dotting the fields around us and increasing the sensation that people measured time differently here.

First impressions were immediately serene and peaceful and this was what served as a magnet—drawing visitors back again and again.

There was something magical about the farm. Wildlife was abundant and there were lots of deer taking advantage of the open, grassy fields. Foxes, raccoons, porcupines and skunks wandered around, somewhat indifferent to us.

Often when we went to town, we passed a male grouse parading around the top of the driveway, where it connected to the road. He puffed his chest out and chortled his love call at our car—he must have been lonely but undiscouraged. I loved watching him drumming for attention but I never noticed any females acknowledging him.

Anyone visiting our farm felt an immediate connection to a more natural world. Something spiritual invited you to take a deep breath as you became one with your surroundings. Details of everything around you were accentuated and there was a sense of belonging. If you were lucky enough, you might see an eagle swooping down to steal a fish from the pond.

People came and were never in a hurry to leave. There was something I couldn't put my finger on, but you felt it every moment you were there.

This was Cynthia's introduction to our home and

our family. She arrived in the early evening and the social worker didn't spend much time offering any advice or directions. School would start in two weeks and the social worker was clear that we were not to enrol her in our local high school as she was entering a special 'Parent Counsellor' program that involved a lot of structure and discipline. The social worker herself was going on vacation for two weeks, but if I had any questions, there was an on-call worker who would help me out.

I gave Cynthia the two-bit tour of our house and showed her to her room. She had little luggage or possessions and I welcomed her to unpack at her own pace. I then left her for a few moments and invited her to join us downstairs when she was ready. Keeping the other kids back to give her time to settle in wasn't easy.

It wasn't long before Maggie and Cynthia made an appearance and started up with the plea to share a room. The united front had formed in record time and I don't think they had hardly exchanged names before deciding they had to give up their privacy and share as much time as possible together.

Maggie had a huge bedroom which could have easily fit several double beds, but space wasn't the issue. I found myself explaining the reasoning for separate rooms, but my audience was unreceptive. Maggie tried to list all the benefits to having Cynthia in her room and their persuasions generally circled around being able to provide companionship, soothe away her anxiety, be supportive and of course be a sympathetic ear.

They would have plenty of opportunity to spend time together but, I insisted Cynthia would have her own room to retreat to whenever she needed her own space. It didn't go down well but it would be a rule that I would never relax, unless of course I got siblings to look after.

I remembered something preacher Charles Spurgeon said: "Begin as you mean to go on, and go on as you began." I thought it would be easier to determine house rules, stick to them and make them apply to everyone. That meant no preferential treat-ment— my kids or visiting family would have the same expectations as foster kids. So much easier to administer and fairer to everyone when there isn't a double standard.

I remembered one of the issues addressed during our training was religion. We were to respect and accommodate individual beliefs, no matter how far removed they were from our own.

Our faith was Protestant, which we loosely followed by attending a nearby part-time church. Because there were only eight or ten parishioners, the church did not maintain its own minister and it was tended by one who looked after several equally small communities. The church held service every other Sunday and we never heard a service longer than twenty minutes, and that included two hymns.

Cynthia had been with us a few days and things were going well. Sunday came three days later and as usual, I told the kids, including my nieces and nephew, to get ready for church. Cynthia stepped forward to tell me she was an atheist and like a plague, every single kid chimed in with the shared affliction.

I knew I was supposed to respect any religious assertion, even if it meant none at all. But I wasn't going to leave them all on their own if my husband and I went off even for half an hour. I managed to persuade them that, because they couldn't be left behind and as it was such a brief service, I was pretty sure they could stifle their religious objections.

Despite their reluctance, they all dressed up nicely and we piled into our old Buick LeSabre, with the exception of my husband, simply because there was no room. I secured promises that there was to be no mockery or giggling during the service and I was proud of them all for making the effort.

We arrived at the church and I know we raised a few eyebrows. This was a very small church and our family of seven almost doubled the congregation.

Everyone behaved through the service and afterwards, several of the parishioners came over to greet the kids. They were the only young people there and the older people seemed quite pleased to see them.

We were soon on our way home and it wasn't long before we turned into our driveway. The upper end of the path was shrouded in a dank canopy of fir trees while the smell of spruce sap pleasantly greeted out senses. A barren landscape of discarded needles insulated sound with its rusty brown carpet dissolving into the distance on both sides of the driveway.

I guess that's why it made it easy for the kids to spot something fluttering on the ground about 30 feet to the right of our car as we crept by. I stopped the car to permit an investigation and as soon as they piled out, shrieks of excitement announced the discovery of a baby bird. It was too young to be out of the nest, and there was no sign of where it could have come from.

The kids were determined to rescue this tiny bundle. I tried to warn them that these things don't often work out. We wouldn't be able to recreate a nest or its missing parents and weren't even sure of the species.

Pleading eyes met mine in the rear-view mirror. I weakened and agreed to try to to keep it alive, but stressed the likelihood that it wouldn't survive very long. I wish my prediction had been less accurate.

As we were pulling up in front of our house, there was a chorus of voices stressing caution. We had two cats, one of which wasn't of concern; but the second could nail a hummingbird in flight. Many mornings I had opened my door to hang out laundry only to find the tiny body of a ruby throated hummingbird on my porch. I had even put a bell on the cat to try and provide a warning, but she taught herself to move without even the slightest tinkle.

Gently, the kids slowly slid out of the back seat with my niece, Sarah, cupping her little cargo close to her chest. They might as well have rang the dinner bell.

What happened next was a blur. Sarah lost her balance, relaxed her grip for just a second, and the fledgling quickly found the ground. I don't know where the cat came from. We had only just pulled up and it was as if she were waiting for us, having some premonition that we carried a treat for her.

My husband arrived quickly and grabbed the cat, but it was too late for the bird.

The cat couldn't be blamed for following its nature, and it was quite taken aback by all the screaming. Sarah had to be consoled that accidents happen and it was just not meant to be.

Each of the kids had been witness to a tragedy, and with long faces, they headed out into the field to bury their friend.

I went inside to get lunch ready and was soon followed by one of the kids.

"We need the Bible."

"What do you mean, you need the Bible?"

"We thought we should do a reading over Speedy's grave."

"Speedy?" I muffled a snort.

"Yeah, that's what we named him and we want to say a few words from the Bible."

I stifled comments about naming a bird Speedy after his untimely death."But you're all atheists..."

"Yeah, but we still need to make it proper."

I gave them the Bible, recommended a few psalms and off they went. It was a solemn occasion.

The lesson here is to never take anything your kids say too seriously. At that young age, ideas about who you are or who you want to be can be very fluid. Cynthia may very well have stuck to her assertion that she was an atheist as she grew up but she also might have floated a few other beliefs before she settled on the one that met her needs. The same with my daughter and nieces and nephew.

I didn't react with fear for their souls when they made their declaration. I didn't think being an atheist was what would represent them into the future. I spent zero thought or effort in trying to dissuade them and decided to let time and a little more life experience help them work it out.

I know I risk sounding preachy, but another one of my fundamentals is that if you keep kids busy, they have less time to get bored and go looking for trouble. It was not unusual for me to pack the kids into the car, maybe take a picnic lunch, and head out for a nearby beach or park.

With the intention of switching up the sombre loss of Speedy, we decided to spend the afternoon at the beach and loaded up bodies, food and blankets. The drive wouldn't last more than 15 minutes and I turned on the radio to the dulcet sounds of the Spice Girls singing 'Wannabe'. This kicked off a com-petition to see who could sing along the loudest.

I've always been able to ignore noise, thank God, as I'm not sure the sounds coming from the back seat could be categorized as singing.

As we pulled into the parking lot facing expansive

sand dunes, a party-like atmosphere had developed. We grabbed a nearby picnic table under a pitched roof, and the girls immediately jumped up on top of the table and tried to mimic a dance routine. Cynthia jumped so high; she literally cracked her head on a beam, but she didn't stop dancing.

The girls and my one lone nephew put a lot of effort into putting a polish on their performance. They were loud and, fortunately, the beach was large and only a few people dotted the warm sands around us.

Eventually the kids settled down and, as I set up our base, took advantage of the gentle waves. Squeals let me know when someone had stepped on a wriggling lobster larval, and hermit crabs were always a source of curiosity, especially to my nieces and nephew, who were inland dwellers from Toronto.

Everything was going well until the girls ran out of the water screaming. Down the beach and off in the distance, an elderly man in his eighties was slowly wading into the water. He wore a thong that did nothing to support his genitals and his flaccid butt cheeks gently lifted and fell with each passing swell.

"You can't be serious!" I said. "It's the Atlantic Ocean!"

They were adamant that they could not share the same water with someone who was swishing their privates around. He was hundreds of yards away but he could have been standing next to them for all the revulsion erupting amongst them. It didn't matter that this was someone very comfortable with who they were, just enjoying a dip on a public beach. Nothing could persuade them to get back into the tainted water.

We had lunch and they fooled around for a while, safely distant from any lapping water that threatened to anoint them with old man germs. Even though the gentleman eventually got out of the water, they weren't going back in.

The ocean had been corrupted on that day but luckily, it wasn't a permanent situation. Future trips didn't keep anyone out of the water and I was probably the only one who could never forget it.

At this time, my sisters' kids flew back home and I do remember her comments on how robust they looked when she picked them up at the airport. "They looked so healthy!" she said excitedly over the phone.

I can remember when they had first arrived at the farm. Loaded in with their luggage were three pairs of roller blades. The closest pavement was a road several miles away and definitely no skate parks for a hundred miles. It had taken them a while to adjust to country life, helping out with looking after our birds, two large gardens and an apple orchard, but they had thrived. It would become a familiar comment I would hear about kids who had the opportunity to spend some time with us.

Our food was home-grown and organic for the most part and there was always plenty of it. It would become a familiar comment I would hear about kids who had the opportunity to spend some time with us. Things were relaxed. I planned frequent activities and we often had fun like water fights and even participated in a well-developed paintball park nearby.

Cynthia had adjusted well to our home and, once my nieces and nephew were gone, it seemed as if the house became larger. Her friendship with my daughter had grown and she also seemed to enjoy philosophical debates with my husband. Wade was generally a quiet person, reluctant to engage others in conversation, but an easy banter flowed between them and furthered an atmosphere of peace and tranquility.

When Cynthia was introduced to our house rules, something came up that still has me shaking my head many years later. Everyone was responsible for doing their own laundry and this standard would apply to kids aged ten and up.

It wasn't that Cynthia had a problem washing her clothes. She shared an issue with my daughter about hanging them on the line. They didn't want to dangle their underwear where everyone could see them.

Our nearest neighbours were a quarter mile away and we were situated in the middle of a 120 acre field. I initially thought this was just a ploy for them to access the dryer because they wanted a shortcut in getting their clothes done. It became an ongoing argument where they preferred drying their inti-mates in their room rather than risk prying eyes violating their privacy.

I still think it was pretty ludicrous, but they were steadfast in their convictions.

With Cynthia feeling comfortable and safe in our home, I encouraged her to share pieces of her life story. I listened quietly and kept comments to a minimum.

I knew the community she came from and I had once had family there. It used to be a lovely village with great people, and we had spent a lot of time there in the past. Things had changed and some of what she told me was so discouraging and heart-breaking. There was a culture there that had brought drugs into the area and, maybe because it was somewhat isolated, it was easier for dealers to climb up on top of youth and take charge.

She told me of one incident when some young guy had done something to irritate one of the local dealers and a bunch of teens gathered behind a closed garage to deal with the lapse. A circle formed around the guy and they used chains to beat him.

I asked why he didn't run away and get help, but there was a resignation to the whole event. He had to take the beating and if he had tried to get away, punishment would have been much worse.

Living in that community had become an absolute nightmare for many, and apathy had created a carpet of complacency. I mourned the loss of a warm, caring community I had known not far in the past.

When Cynthia first came to us, it was made clear that she would be moving on to a special program called 'Parent Counsellors'. It would be a home with a couple who would be devoted to helping her develop structure and discipline. Schooling would be strictly monitored and she would have to achieve and maintain her grades at a certain level. She would attend regular psychiatric appointments, take what medications were recommended and live in a closely monitored environment. She could have no contact with anyone from her village and would also be restricted from social activities. She could very well be in this program for a year before she could even think about going home. Her parents would also undergo some counselling to make sure things stayed on track when she returned.

Cynthia was 15 and had officially been diagnosed with Oppositional Defiant Disorder and Attention Deficit Disorder. She had become impossible for her parents to deal with and placing her in this intense program was designed to bring her and her parents to a level of co-operation and control that would make the family whole.

And Cynthia was having none of it.

The social worker who had dropped her off was still on vacation and, although school was starting, Cynthia was not to attend in our area. She was to wait until things had been set up with her Parent Counsellors and then start school where that was going to be.

My own daughter, who had started the new academic year, was chit chatting with Cynthia about goings-on in school. Being left out was upsetting for her and she pressed me to find out why she couldn't attend with Maggie.

I called Social Services, and her temporary worker told me to go ahead and enrol her despite not knowing how long it might be for.

This made Cynthia quite happy and, despite all the issues she struggled with, nothing interfered with her behaviour at our school. For that matter, Cynthia hadn't presented any problems in our home.

However, letting her go to school resulted in my first reprimand from Children's Aid. When Cynthia's social worker got back from vacation, she paid me a visit and was more than a little irritated with me. I told her I was not confused with her directions, but that I felt it was causing Cynthia even more stress to be excluded from what other teens were doing. I thought getting permission from Children's Aid made it okay, but apparently not.

The social worker reminded me that this was a temporary situation for us, and that Cynthia would soon be moving on. She would be allowed to continue with our local school for the time being and I learned to never get involved in a situation where one social worker might differ with another. They would work it out between them and, even though I received two different sets of directions, I really needed to stay out of it as much as possible.

Cynthia had had problems dealing with stress in the past, and one of the things she resorted to was self-harming. I had several talks with her and, along with my husband, tried to get her to recognize any warning signs that things were about to get out of control. Stresses and frustrations about what was happening in her life could be triggered by something simple.

I was very pleased with her one day when she approached me and told me she was feeling that pressure that usually resulted in the need to hurt herself. My husband and I had been trained to make sure we got professional help immediately and that meant a trip to the ER in Truro, 40 minutes away.

I took off with Cynthia and, during the drive, continued to talk with her. I really thought it was a big step for her to come forward and try and deal with this before something happened.

It was late evening when we arrived and we soon found ourselves sitting in a waiting room watching the time tick by. After a couple of hours we were ushered into an examination room. Cynthia appeared outwardly calm but still insisted she felt on the edge of something. This feeling of anxiety without knowing the source could build to the point of an explosion and she was eager to get help.

Eventually, a young doctor wandered in. I asked Cynthia if she wanted to be alone but she preferred I stay. She sat on the examination table and I was across the room from her when the doctor introduced himself. His next words are branded into my brain.

"So, what happens to be your particular problem?"

To say he might have sneered would be harsh. But

there was an odour of contempt that immediately rubbed Cynthia the wrong way. She looked at me and her eyes were pleading. There was absolutely no air of compassion or interest coming from the doctor and Cynthia looked at the door before looking back at me. She wanted to escape.

"Do you want to go home?" I said.

"Yes."

And with that we walked out.

She didn't have a life-threatening injury, but she was there because she felt she was at risk. I found myself staggered by the doctor's insensitivity and indifference. How could he be so callous? He must have some training in dealing with emotional trauma but he left it back on a shelf before he walked in.

I had the feeling that if Cynthia had actually harmed herself subsequent to the ER visit, their official response would have been that they had offered professional assistance. But they sure as hell did not.

If someone had told me I was wasting my time to take a troublesome teen to the ER late at night, I would have argued that there must be something they could do to help. What if she had been suicidal? She wasn't and, fortunately, she hadn't taken a piece of glass to her arm or legs as she had done in the past.

I had heard Cynthia complain before about how she didn't feel she was getting help. This doctor treated her like a petulant child. Was this a professional response? Nothing in her manner was uncooperative or defiant. We both resigned ourselves that this had been a waste of time. I knew she was not about to share anything with this doctor and there was no point hanging around.

We headed home and my husband was equally shocked at our exercise in futility. We were on our own in dealing with Cynthia's emotional struggles, and she was definitely alone in this particular instance.

The plan in place for Cynthia involved a series of appointments with a psychiatrist, and these were already underway before she came to stay with us. It was now my job to make sure she attended on time.

The first time I escorted her; I spent a few minutes talking with the doctor about how she had been doing. I used a natural consequence method of motivating kids to stay within our house rules. There were rewards for jobs well done and, when things weren't up to scratch, I sought out something that mattered and placed a restriction on it. This could mean less time on the computer, phone or video games—it all depended on the individual.

This was working for me but I can't take all the credit. Kids often behave better for someone else than they do for you. Have you ever taken your family to dinner at someone else's house to find at the end of the meal, your teenager is happily washing dishes, smiling and laughing as they offer to do anything? How it grates on you when you know wild horses couldn't drag them to your sink! I think some of that was in play at our house and helped Cynthia to put more effort in following my rules.

I didn't have anything negative to report on her and the doctor found this intriguing. So interesting, in fact, that he decided it might be beneficial if I met with Cynthia's parents.

A meeting was set up and I drove in one afternoon while Cynthia was in school. We met at the board room at the Children's Aid office, along with Cynthia's social worker.

I was really pleased to get to know her parents and I found them sincere and down-to-earth. They were both quiet but expressed their appreciation to me for looking after their girl.

The father was small in stature and had poor health, which left him physically limited from doing much of anything. Her mother sat with hunched shoulders; she reminded me of someone who wanted to disappear within themselves.

I found myself sympathizing with their situation as they detailed their history and how they found themselves in over their heads with Cynthia. They talked about how she had taken control of their home. They lived in a house trailer and I learned that, after Cynthia had filled her room and refused to clean it, she had moved out into the living room and took over that space as well. There was no negotiating with her—she raised hell when confronted and the parents had given up.

Cynthia seemed particularly hateful towards her mother and often verbally abused her. This was a side I had not seen, nor would I have put up with it.

Having met Cynthia's parents, I felt a real satisfaction that I was a part of something designed to help this family heal and get back together again. I understood the need for the parents to develop more structure and apply strategies in dealing with Cynthia's behaviour. I still found the Parent Counsellor program hard core and very intense but those in charge felt that this was the route for Cynthia to go in order to bring her in line.

A few days after meeting Cynthia's parents, I was asked to bring her in to meet the family designated to be her Parent Counsellors. I wasn't supposed to be a part of this, but she requested I be in attendance and Children's Aid was trying to be accommodating and show how flexible they were. It was all part of giving the appearance that she had some say in what was going on when, in fact, she had no control at all.

The couple we were introduced to were amiable and benign on the surface. Both were mature and retired from their careers—he had a military background and she had been in the education system. They would be available to devote a lot of attention on Cynthia and her issues.

The gentleman was very cheerful and chatty and they both described their home life as a friendly and secure environment. They were welcoming and offered a healthy, happy place where they would work closely with her to make sure her schooling experience would be optimized and her responsibilities at home designed to teach her confidence, self-reliance and responsibility.

Cynthia begged for more time with us.

I wasn't running a holiday haven for youth, but things had been going well. Eventually, I would learn that children who have experienced trauma will usually keep it buried until they find themselves in a safe environment. Whatever happened to them will then rise to the surface and the child will be ready to address it.

Part of dealing with Cynthia's past involved making sure damage had not resulted from the sexual assault that had taken place. She refused to be involved in any criminal charges, but after three weeks with us, she finally agreed to have a full medical examination. It was decided I would take her to her family GP and I had to be present for the examination.

It was my first experience dealing with a medical professional who made no attempt to mask his contempt for me or the foster care program. I'm not sure which governed his attitude. I had no choice in the decision to remove Cynthia from her home and I had met and genuinely liked her parents.

He refused to speak to me, and when talking to Cynthia, he grabbed a chair, turned it around and conducted his interview with his back to me. He never once acknowledged I was even in the room. His body language spoke volumes. Perhaps he was expressing sympathy and support for the parents.

Results of the appointment were good and no damage evident from her experience. As quiet as it was, it had been a milestone in Cynthia's moving forward with her life.

Children's Aid was getting impatient with Cynthia's reluctance to step into the Parent Counsellor program. The initial proposal of "When you're ready" wasn't being offered anymore and, finally, they gave her one last week with us, with a moving-on deadline.

It's not like we didn't know it was going to happen. But she had become close friends with my daughter and they planned to stay in touch.

It was during Cynthia's last week that an interesting experience occurred. We were on our way to town, driving down that long, dusty road, when the kids spotted something in the ditch.

I stopped the car and realized we were watching a fox making her way through the dead grass and bushes. She was thin and her fur patchy. It looked like she might have mange but, in her mouth, she carried a grouse. I was relieved to realize it was not the handsome fellow who was installed at the top of our driveway.

The kids were very upset at her condition and a momentum developed where they believed something had to be done. I tried to tell them there wasn't any group or agency responsible for checking out skinny foxes. They persisted. This wasn't right and they were fuelled by my apathy.

We got home and I steered them in the direction of our local Lands and Forests provincial office. I decided this would be a learning opportunity, so I insisted they make the call themselves. I can still see

Cynthia on the phone with Maggie at her side while I listen from the other room.

The results were quite predictable. They successfully got a hold of a forest ranger and didn't exactly like his responses.

"What do you mean, we need to let nature take its course?!"

His explanation that the fox may not have been injured and was successfully able to hunt wasn't the level of concern they were looking for. He also offered that her thinness might have been the result of her caring for a brood of kits. No one was available to save a fox that didn't need saving.

The girls were outraged at what they perceived as his insensitivity. They hung up after loudly expressing their frustrations. It didn't help that I agreed with the forest ranger and tried to get them to realize the reality of the situation.

Not everything has a happy ending and not all problems have a resolution. It was something I wanted them to accept in spite of their enthusiasm and determination to right what they thought was wrong. Things don't always get fixed.

The week progressed and Cynthia's departure day arrived. I hoped we could stay in touch, but that would prove to be unfeasible according to regulations.

I'm not an emotional person, so it's not as if I was teary at her leaving us. I thought we had made a connection and I was anxious to see what progress would be made to make her whole again. I wanted more than anything to see her back with her family and living a healthy, positive life.

In the years to follow, I would occasionally have some contact with Cynthia and I believed we were both disappointed in the course of action Children's Aid took on her behalf. I don't know what the right answer would have been, but I do know that, the more I learned about Parent Counsellors, the more reason I would have to disapprove of and suspect their methods.

As with the pointless trip to the ER and the response to the skinny fox trying to survive, I found myself wondering if there really was something or someone out there that would help the Cynthias.

Time would tell and, in a few years, I would have my answer.

2: Beyond this point there be monsters

I heard about Roberta long before I met her. Her infamy preceded her like the smell of dust precedes a good rain storm. Another lost soul was brought into the system and refused to be stuffed into any mould.

She had been sent away to a youth residential facility in a desperate attempt at bringing her behaviour under control. To say she was oppositional was an understatement. She had already run through some local foster parents, who had deemed her to be beyond what was on offer there.

Youth workers at the facility were becoming burned out by her conduct and they approached us to see if we could be a respite home for them. It would be a long weekend of four days and I have to say I was apprehensive.

They gave me some background on Roberta's family. They were, at the outset, upstanding and well thought of in the community. Something had happened early in Roberta's life and had festered until she was at the point she was now. Anger had been escalating in this child for nine years.

There were suspicions about what might have happened, but nothing actionable, and in the meantime, there was a furious girl who had decided she would never cooperate with anyone or anything.

The day Roberta was scheduled to come to our home, she crawled out a window of the residential facility and climbed up onto the roof. There she sat, waving at traffic and refusing to come in.

Fire department and police arrived, but to no immediate avail. She eventually came down, punctuating once again that everything had to be on her terms.

Roberta was delivered to us mid-afternoon on a Thursday and she was quiet, with downcast eyes and furtive looks. She was a pretty girl and I especially remember how pink her cheeks were. She looked like an absolute darling, the kind of girl you would expect to see in the English countryside, picking wild flowers in the fields.

I think it took half an hour before things blew up. I can't even remember the issue, but I suddenly found myself leaning over her as she sat in a chair. Her eyes flashed and her lips were tightened across her teeth in a slight snarl.

"You will never tell me what to do in my home!"

She was fast at getting my goat, achieving my flash point at record speed. I remember being so angry and not dealing with the situation very well. I know intimidation is not a positive means of communication but it was all I could do to not flip into a lunatic. All I remember is that she had immediately tried to take control and I was having none of it.

But I also realized her behaviour was rooted in something even she might not be aware of. I am a control freak and giving in to her was not something I could do. I found myself retreating.

There were a few other kids with us at that time, younger in years and each with their own issues. I counted on our farm to exude its peaceful charm and, after some thought, I decided to try an unorthodox way to slip by Roberta's defences. I was determined that Roberta would melt into the fabric of our home, even if for a brief period.

I had recently read a book by Monty Roberts, *The Man Who Listens to Horses*. I was intrigued by the method a horse herd deals with a colt that decides to misbehave and tear it up around the herd. They respond by shutting the young horse out, turning them away and refusing them access to the protection of the herd. In the wild, this is a very dangerous situation and the colt is suddenly at risk from predators.

The colt will then lower its head, showing submission and beg for acceptance. In this manner, they learn consequences to their behaviour.

As outrageous as it sounds, I decided to treat Roberta like a colt. I cut her off from the herd.

She would never comply with a command or order from anyone. I decided I wouldn't tell her to do anything. She was not a part of our group and would have to prove herself to be accepted. I would make everything her choice, but I would manipulate her every step of the way.

For example, dinner was soon set on the table and I knew that if I told her to take a seat and eat, she would stay in the living room just out of spite.

"We're all going to have supper now. You're welcome to join us." I extended an invitation, not an order. With that I walked away, the rest of the kids followed and she found herself alone.

A few seconds later, she walked in and took a seat at the table. I didn't let my excitement show and, instead, acted like she wasn't even there and paid her no attention.

Meal done, the other kids wandered off to do chores or have some quiet time. This was my next hurdle.

I expected everyone under our roof to share in household chores and this was mandatory. Recently, one of the foster kids had left and there was a hole in the roster. We usually had a weekly meeting to discuss things, including allocation of work and any complaints someone might have. I wanted Roberta to participate but without her realizing that she was.

She was sitting quietly in the corner of the living room, and I pulled everyone together in a rough circle around her, but as if our placement was accidental. A few of the kids were interested in trading chores with others just for a change, and I helped work out the scheduling. At the end of the meeting, I found myself without someone to empty the dishwasher. I acted confused at this development and, ignoring Roberta, I asked if anyone had any suggestions on how we could fix this.

I was shocked when she spoke up and said she could empty it. "Are you sure?"

I know I manipulated this scenario, but Roberta had freely offered to take on a chore, something that every other child was expected to do in my home. Did this not indicate that she actually wanted to be a part of something? She had been induced to offer herself into our little mob by stepping up and accepting a chore. This brought her into a level footing with everyone else there and it had happened without demands or frustration.

I was very proud of her. While my brain was doing cartwheels, I thanked her for being generous. I was pretty sure that if I made any kind of fuss, she might back out, so I opted instead to continue treating her like a horse who was now rewarded by being accepted into the herd.

Some of the kids staying with us were special needs, and I filled Roberta in on what their issues were and how I expected everyone to treat them. Again, I didn't tell her what to do, I just told her what we were doing and how we handled certain issues.

Roberta glided in to our little school like a shoal of fish with their noses all pointed upstream, and let the water flow gently past her. I continued to be careful how I worded requests around her. I didn't directly demand anything, but if I suggested I needed help with something, she would often volunteer.

I gave her some knitting needles and wool and she quickly found a pattern for a teddy bear. When she wasn't playing games or busy with something else, she was intensely working out the tricky parts of the pattern and was completely absorbed by it. She appeared to be at peace, for as brief a period as it was. I happily reported her cooperation to her social worker.

The four days passed in a flash and she was picked up to be returned to the home for troubled youth. I actually didn't expect to see her again, or at least not for a long time, but I was surprised at how fast I found her back with us again.

Roberta had appointments with psychiatrists and probation officers in Truro, at some distance from her group home. It was recommended that when she had such appointments, she should stay a while with us and let me escort her.

It turned out she had many appointments. I had the slight impression this may have been orchestrated to relieve youth facility staff. They were busy enough without losing a staff member for hours escorting Roberta to appointments.

There were always opportunities for power struggles between Roberta and me. Treating her like a horse wasn't always the logical path.

Children's Aid rules were that I had to accompany her physically, making sure she made it to each appointment: in the door and sitting in a waiting room until she was called in and the door was shut.

The first time I took her to see her probation officer, I pulled up outside the building and she tried to tell me I wasn't going up with her. It wasn't unusual for her to try and call the shots and she shouldn't have been surprised by my response.

"Any time you have a need and I have a need; my needs will always supersede yours. You have to see your probation officer and I have to make sure you get there.".

"Well, I'm not going with you," she said defiantly.

"I'm going in, and you better figure out how you plan to get there. Missing the appointment isn't an option."

I think, in her own way, she won that one when she declared she was going to use the back stairs. This was really hard for me. Normally, I would need to have eyes on her because she was always capable of causing a commotion.

I swallowed my fear and told her I'd meet her upstairs. I took the elevator up and was so apprehensive until I saw her walk through the door. What a relief! We were downtown, and if she had decided to make a break for it, she could have been gone in a flash.

The probation officer asked to speak to me briefly to inquire how things were going. I had no complaints. Her appointment was less than half an hour and we were soon on our way back home.

Roberta was slowly becoming more and more comfortable with our home. She still battled with the knitting pattern for the teddy bear, but refused to give in. She could be a very determined young lady, and this characteristic could do her well.

The weeks she came to us sometimes involved a

weekend, and during one of her visits, I loaded up the car and headed into town to do some shopping. I decided to drop by our local thrift store and give the kids some money to fool around with.

Roberta had never been to a thrift store and she was disdainful of anyone who bought second hand stuff. Cynthia was still with us at this point and an absolute demon when it came to thrift shopping. She was addicted to what we referred to as 'old man golf clothes'. She sought out the most hideous plaid pants and baggy golf shirts and her enthusiasm in the hunt was contagious.

I hung back by the entrance checking out some stuff, and was interrupted by Cynthia's squeals. Down the aisle, she was waving a pair of yellow/green plaid pants like the leader of a victory parade.

Then I realized Roberta was no longer with me. Way down another aisle, she was elbow deep in a pile of sweaters. Her snobbish manner had evaporated and she ploughed through several bins in record time.

Then I made a surprise discovery of my own. I came across a pair of peach satin underwear in my size and had no idea Victoria's Secret even made briefs for larger women.

Everyone eventually made their way to the checkout—Cynthia with her traditional old man clothes, Roberta with a top and some jeans and two other children with their treasures. All the purchases went into one large bag and, because I didn't want my underwear mixed up with their stuff, I tucked it into my purse.

It had been a productive afternoon, so I decided to treat us to pancakes at a local establishment. We had an enjoyable meal and the place was almost empty for a Sunday afternoon. It was when we were done and I went to pay that things got a little out of hand. As I reached into my purse for my wallet, the peach satin underwear poked up like a cobra rising out of a basket. As I tried to stuff it back down, Cynthia grabbed it and waved it in front of Roberta's face.

She screamed and they were off. Ducking and diving, Roberta tried desperately to avoid being tagged by the underwear. I kept asking for quiet and the return of my garment but to no avail.

I apologized to the restaurant staff and paid as fast as I could to make a hasty exit.

I think the thing that got me most was how aloof Roberta was when we initially went to the thrift store and how, two hours later, she was being chased by old lady briefs and laughing so hard she could hardly stand upright.

Cracking through Roberta's shell was an incremental process totally without direction or strategy. Another one of her issues was that she had not allowed herself to be touched in any way by anyone. She had not enjoyed a warm hug or reassuring hand on her shoulder since she was quite young, but something inside of her was craving human contact.

I found this out one day when I was trying to pass from the living room to the dining room and Roberta blocked my path. Arms and legs spread eagle in the doorway, she presented a challenge to me, knowing I couldn't grab her to move her out of my way. She wore an impish grin as she watched me struggle with the puzzle she presented.

I suddenly hit on a solution that I thought was brilliant. I couldn't put my hands on her, but, by turning around, bending over and backing up, I could push arse first into her body. She surrendered her post, hesitating long enough to briefly wrap her arms around me as she pretended to hang on to the door frame. She giggled as she let go and her cheeks were flushed in that brilliant pink only she could display.

This became a ritual for Roberta, and she often obstructed my passage, expectant of my butt- first attack which she loudly protested in disgust. I think this was her way of satisfying a yearning that had been brewing for years. It had to be on her terms, of course, and she would never admit she needed physical contact, but there it was.

Roberta was spending less and less time at the group home and more time with us. The goal was still to reunite her with her family and a lot of resources were involved in making the family whole again.

I was still required to deliver her to appointments and one day I had to escort her to see her psychiatrist. The office was in a building attached to our main hospital that had its own entrance with a big, glass-fronted lobby.

Roberta may have been getting along well with us,

but she wasn't beyond pulling off any stunts. I found her challenges more playful than a serious attempt at disruption. She was ahead of me going into the building and she suddenly turned and grabbed onto the door, not letting me in. I tried pulling but she was quite strong and kept her grip, refusing me access.

Well, this is embarrassing, I thought. No one was around but that would probably change soon. I knew Roberta to be very determined and who knows how long she could have held out.

I had a brain storm (rather a brain fart) and turned around and pretended I was about to moon her. Squealing, she let go of the door and ran, flapping her hands like a chicken.

I arrived at the doctor's office moments after Roberta and we quietly awaited the summons. Again, the doctor asked how everything was going and I shared some details about some of the things we got up to. The doctor was interested in how I addressed some of Roberta's behaviour. I didn't dare admit to him that I was treating her like a horse. I was pretty sure it wouldn't have been found in any treatment protocols available to mental health professionals.

The psychiatrist found what was happening in our home very interesting and suggested we all get together in a session with the family and have an exchange. I wasn't letting Roberta call the shots and she was still oppositional on occasion but somehow, we were making it work. The doctor felt there could be some benefit to meeting the parents and talking about our home life.

This made me so uncomfortable. I was a complete stranger to these people, yet here I was looking after their child and having to share how I responded to some problems Roberta presented.

It wasn't long before we heard from the psychiatrist's office about a meeting with Roberta's parents and her social worker. It was arranged for a time when all the kids were in school and I drove in with hopes that something positive would come from sharing our experiences with Roberta. Again, I chose not to reveal how I had initially treated her like a wayward colt.

We were all introduced and, while Roberta's father was immediately open and friendly, her mother was not. He offered some details about Roberta's earlier years and how things had deteriorated to the point where things had become physical. Fearful of what could happen, they had placed Roberta in care and she had been receiving counselling, with progress being slower than they would like.

The psychiatrist wanted me to express how I handled her defiance and did not give in to her demand for control. Nothing I did was sophisticated in any way—just old-fashioned common sense and natural consequences for unacceptable behaviour. Roberta could be difficult but not impossible.

It was at this point I realized Roberta's mother was staring at me with a dead, fish- eyed glare. She had contributed nothing to the discussion and appeared to be indifferent to any commentary. Her face betrayed no emotion and I found myself thinking about the book Joan Crawford's daughter wrote, *Mommy Dearest*.

There was a bit of malice peeking through the curtains for her eyes and I had the distinct impression she wasn't about to accept any advice I might offer even though I didn't try to portray our home as a Utopian haven for wayward teens. It was clear she resented the changes that had started to take place in Roberta and the observations the psychiatrist highlighted.

The father's revelations at the beginning of the meeting had brushed over an incident that might have happened involving the teenage son of her mother's best friend. At this disclosure, the mother turned and directed her quiet fury towards her husband. I had the impression this was a narrative everyone was well aware of, but that having it laid out before me was not something the mother willingly suffered. It was information she desperately tried to strangle and I was not in the 'need to know' class.

I got the distinct impression that something had happened and Roberta's mother had dismissed it. I wouldn't say she didn't deal with it, but not to the point of reporting it or having her daughter checked out. Roberta was five years old at the time.

I now found myself struggling to contain my own anger. Her best friend's son molests her little daughter and her primary focus was to make sure it was kept quiet so as not to embarrass her or her husband. And here we are, nine years later, and Roberta may not have pinpointed the source of her anger but she did know it had something to do with her mother. Her mother had jettisoned her own daughter just to preserve her social status.

And there she was, across the table, glaring at me with narrowed eyes. Is it guilt that makes people project their outrage at others? Her little girl had been permanently damaged but, thankfully, she could still live in a community where no one was whispering behind her back.

I left the meeting feeling like I needed a shower.

Roberta continued to make our home her second residence and we saw her often. Christmas was approaching and the teddy bear she was knitting was slowly taking shape. One of the things I always participated in before Christmas was volunteering at the local food bank for the month leading up to the holidays. I had always involved my own children in the past and I saw no reason why I shouldn't include the foster children in helping out in their community.

I was usually concerned with paperwork, signing in applicants for a Christmas hamper, tracking volunteer hours or doing up court reports for anyone who was doing community service. One of the local supporters of the food bank was a franchise of a national pastry/coffee shop and daily they dropped off day-old muffins, donuts, bagels and cookies. Some of this stuff came in crushed and usually went to the dumpster, but sometimes I took some home with me to give to my chickens and ducks. They absolutely loved the stuff that was broken up and I often had a bag defrosting on the cupboard, waiting for me to scatter across the lawn. Chickens and turkeys stayed in the coop and had their treats delivered there but ducks and guineas roomed free around the property.

Something I liked to do every Christmas was to build a gingerbread house. It would usually end up more candy than gingerbread, but it was a bit of creative fun that we all got to participate in. I would build the basic house form and occasionally got fancy by adding a porch or some gabled windows.

I showed the kids how to make stained glass windows with crushed suckers and encouraged them to make their own creations. It was always a work in progress and would take upwards of a week to complete.

We usually used sliced almonds as roof shingles and there were always pathways and a chimney to make with the candy-coated chocolate rocks. There were little Christmas trees to paint and decorate and little wreaths to hang.

I had the kids take turns with different jobs, and for the younger ones it was free-styling with their own candy designs.

We were all proud of the house and had it boldly displayed in the dining room until well after Christmas, when we would then have a ceremony to destroy it. I remember early days in the New Year having a cup of tea and trying to maneuver odd shapes of gingerbread into my cup. The candy was usually the first bits to disappear.

It was shortly after Christmas that I received a checkup visit from Roberta's social worker. These were all pretty informal and Children's Aid was always looking to confirm needs were being met and if there was anything else we might need to help out.

Everything was fine, but as she was leaving the social worker made a strange inquiry. "By the way, it's been reported you are feeding the foster children from food obtained from the food bank."

"What?!" I was so caught off guard.

I explained I wasn't a client of the food bank and certainly didn't get food boxes from them. We had put in some time doing volunteer work there and I begged for details from the social worker. I was told that I was apparently feeding donuts and muffins to the kids which I obtained from the food bank.

Suddenly I remembered those snake eyes glaring at me across a boardroom table when I first met Roberta's parents. Roberta's mother was still simmering at my involvement in the minutia of her torrid family past. She was out to get me anyway she could and filing a complaint with Children's Aid was her shot across the bow. Roberta had had a family visit recently and must have mentioned the garbage stuff I was getting to feed the poultry.

Roberta's mother lobbed grenades from the comfort and security of her home; the telephone was her weapon of choice and nothing was off limits. Nothing would come of her allegations, but I couldn't help feeling I had been violated in my own home.

We were now several months into our adventures

with Roberta and one of the things that I was learning about children in care was that the more comfortable and secure they became, the more likely it was a past trauma would surface.

With Roberta, we first saw this when she admitted to me that in the past, she had run away from homes and had broken into cottages to find safety for the night. I told her she needed to let her social worker know, who then passed it on to local RCMP and they came out to interview her. It wasn't with a mind to laying on any charges but more to clear their books with resolving some open break and enter cases.

They were very professional, of course, and I had to stay during their interview, which was another eye-opening experience. They approached it with a mix of 'you shouldn't have done this' and 'we're glad you're telling us about it now'. This was another new experience for me, and of course my focus was on making sure Roberta felt safe disclosing everything she had done, which had included some property damage.

They made sure she understood that if she wasn't already on probation for other acts, she could very well have been charged with these incidents. They did thank her for coming forward and it was all wrapped up within an hour.

Several months later the social worker came out for a visit and a chat that Roberta had requested. Attempts had been made in the past to find out Roberta's recollections involving the teenage son of her mother's friend. She had not been co-operative, but now things had changed. Roberta was ready to talk.

After getting some information, the social worker told us both it was not too late to take legal action against what was now a full-grown man. The social worker detailed the court proceedings and how Roberta would have to testify to everything that had happened to her.

There were sparks flashing in Roberta's eyes and through a clenched jaw she said yes.

Again, I found myself dropping through a door to another world. The social worker knew her stuff and immediately set up a new appointment to start preparing Roberta for court. She didn't need the parents' permission to file charges against the young man. I wondered about the parents' responsibilities and their failure to protect Roberta, but I guess pursuing that wouldn't have gone far in trying to reconcile the family.

The next meeting between the social worker and Roberta was intense. I had to be present as a support person, and we isolated ourselves in a part of the house for privacy. Roberta had to be able to describe in detail everything she could remember, and learn what to expect as challenges from a defence lawyer.

Roberta responded to everything clearly and was fantastic at keeping her emotions in check. She had waited for this for many years and now was her chance at a justice too long denied. I found it hard to listen to everything, but Roberta was strong enough for us both.

It took over an hour, as the social worker described the court procedures again. She acted so matter of fact about the whole thing—something she had been through too many times herself.

When the coaching and orientation were complete, I felt the strain and Roberta must have been wiped out.

Roberta would move on to realize the justice she was due, in no part thanks to her mother. As in too many of these cases, the punishment was inadequate, but the family was so much farther along with the healing process after the trial had concluded.

Roberta continued to bounce back to us for a little while longer, and I was always happy to see her. Somehow, she had managed to reconcile what had happened at last. I can't say what her relationship with her mother was like.

Life is so much easier when we learn to forgive, and this must have been a big ask for Roberta. I don't know if I could have been so generous under the same circumstances.

3: Desperate women

Linda came to us when we were already sharing our home with Roberta part-time, Kimberley full-time, and had a few other children in our care with various circumstances. Other foster parents had warned me that Children's Aid would try to pack my house with kids, but that didn't intimidate me.

I grew up in a family of eight and my mother was often ill and unable to look after us. I was the oldest, and it fell to me and my younger sisters to care for our even-younger siblings, do housework and, from the age of twelve, cook meals for the family. A busy dinner table with lots of chatter was like gentle music in my ears.

If I walked through the house and found a kid in each room occupying themselves with their own interests, then I felt the home was well used. Lots of bodies around me were comforting to my soul and excess noise did not disturb or distract me. So, the threat of an overcrowded house didn't put me off. It was encouraging to me that we were filling a need and, I hoped, offering some solace to troubled young people.

I don't remember the particulars that delivered

Linda into our care. My priority in receiving a new member of the household was to make them as comfortable as possible.

Linda arrived as an outsider, as everyone initially is, but in some ways, she desperately tried to remain so. I had to question her state of mind when, immediately upon arrival, she told me she had seen a wolf out in the field, watching her as she came down the driveway.

I tried to tell her we have no wolves in our province but she insisted one was waiting for her here. She couldn't be swayed and even added that it was her spirit animal. (She was not indigenous.)

I thought perhaps Linda was feeling especially vulnerable and in need of protection. Maybe she saw this wolf because she wanted to believe it was there to keep her safe.

Some of the kids started to tease her about it and I shut that down. I know it was unusual, but I thought the comfort it brought her outweighed the possibility that this was an unhealthy hallucination.

I'm not exactly sure of the rationale, but Linda's mother had shaved off her daughter's eyebrows before she was taken into care. Maybe it was an effort at something a little more exotic but the result effectively stripped her of any attempt at expression. I wouldn't have guessed how significant eyebrows are in helping people gauge someone's impressions or punctuate an emotion.

Linda didn't know how to create a look on the blank slate left where her eyebrows used to be, and she declined any offers of assistance from me or the other girls staying with us. I guess this was her mother's purview, and it would have to wait till she was back in her care for the project to be completed. In the meantime, I had to watch out for anyone making fun of her.

Linda was 14 and carried a lot of anxiety with her. She was quick to take offence and often had to be placated and assured that she was not under attack.

On a positive note, she made a dramatic decision to quit smoking and threw her cigarettes into the wood stove shortly after arriving. She was really pleased at breaking her dependency and she immediately called her mother to share this triumph. Her mother insisted on speaking to me and I tried to decline but she persisted.

As soon as I took the phone, the mother started telling me how upsetting this all was for Linda. She went on to try to persuade me that I had to drive all the way to her home to pick up another pack of cigarettes for her. She presented her daughter as someone who couldn't function without this anchor and I started to get a clearer picture of where some of Linda's problems originated.

Linda's home was over an hour away, but that was not the issue. It was absolutely preposterous that I aid her mother in maintaining Linda's addiction. Insisting a 14-year-old couldn't live without nicotine was ludicrous, but my refusal to participate wasn't going well. Things started to deteriorate quickly and I terminated the call.

Now Linda was convinced she had made a mistake and retreated to her room crying because she was trapped without a crutch to lean on. Linda would have been fine if her mother hadn't told her she couldn't do it.

I wondered if this was more about her mother's need to cripple Linda than it was about helping her cope in a stressful situation.

A few days later, I was chatting with Linda in the kitchen when she mentioned her older sister, possibly 16, was being made to stay with a friend of her mother's boyfriend. He was in his seventies and this was an overnight stay. I questioned how safe her sister could be in this kind of arrangement and Linda interpreted this as an attack on her family.

It didn't matter how diplomatically I tried to express my concern., Linda was on the defensive and things escalated no matter how hard I tried to calm her. Without warning, she turned and ran out the door, screaming and flailing her arms like a headless chicken as she lit out across the fields.

I watched through the kitchen window and got the distinct impression she thought I was going to run after her and bring her back. The drama was a little more than I cared to indulge so I turned instead and continued preparing lunch.

She was back quicker than I expected and acted as if nothing had happened. I let her know I wasn't going to be drawn into the vortex of her highly volatile emotions. She then calmly walked away to join the others playing video games in the living room.

Linda had an unusual habit of asking for things and then rejecting them. We had a freezer full of stuff I was able to obtain from a local food pro- cessing plant, and battered mozzarella sticks was one of the items the kids often picked out for a snack. Linda asked to have some and my only stipu- lation was that you eat what you take.

She filled up a cookie sheet and I asked her to make sure she could eat them all. She was quite con- fident when she put the tray into the oven. She didn't even get halfway through what she had heated up and, with no one else interested, the rest went into the garbage. I wasn't happy about the waste.

We had occasion to visit some friends in a nearby town and, as guests, we were offered a plate of sweets which included some homemade rum balls. Linda had to have one even after I warned her, they might not taste the way she imagined. She immedi- ately spit it out in front of our hostess and she came over to me, whispering that she didn't like it.

Then, when the same plate was passed around again, she picked up another rum ball and again spit it out. I reprimanded her for taking something she already knew she didn't like and told her to leave them alone. She then went into a corner and pouted for the remainder of the visit, and I was fine with it.

Another incident took place when I managed to get my hands on a bunch of marzipan and we de- cided to try to incorporate the tasty paste into a batch of sugar cookies. Linda took a large portion of the marzipan and heaped it over some cookie dough and I told her the result could be a little overpowering with the almond flavour. They were supposed to be decorating the cookies, but Linda's creative touch was to put a big blob on top which melted when baked and looked unappetizing.

Then after making her cookies, she refused to eat them, saying, "They didn't taste right." This was infuriating, and her refusal to take direction was beginning to wear thin.

Several weeks after we welcomed Linda into our home, one of the other girls approached me and told me Linda thought my husband was 'creepy'.

Wade was usually quiet and not that involved in the day-to-day happenings with the foster children. He was more of a support person for me and stayed in the background unless needed.

There had been occasions when he would take a group of kids to a nearby watering hole, where he would fill barrels with water for our gardens. The kids took advantage by having a nice cooling dip in the stream and sometimes they even did a little fishing.

Anytime one of the kids had a project that involved science or they just wanted to build something, he was there to help in his calm, easy-going manner. This seemed to throw kids off guard as many of them had experienced men who were loud, aggressive and often violent.

Linda wasn't familiar with a man who didn't try to dominate conversations or control activities at every level. Unfortunately, she interpreted his placid demeanour as weird and eerie.

It was approaching Christmas and school had been interrupted for the holidays. I was taking my little crew with me several days a week to help out at the food bank as they gave out their Christmas hampers. It was a very busy time and most of my kids were teens whose youth and energy were much appreciated.

I wanted the children to see all sides of the process, the families in need and thankful for what they received, the donors showing up at the door with food and cash, the volunteers themselves who came from every walk of life, and how they could give of themselves and be a part of a community that looked after its own.

The volunteer coordinator had placements for everyone and assigned Linda to look after the butter table—yes, a table where she made sure the right amount of butter went into the different colour-coded boxes. It wasn't more than an hour before she was brought to me at the sign-in table and left for me to take care of. Apparently, someone had spoken to her in a way she didn't like and she had not reacted well. Basically, she got kicked off the butter table and banned from the kitchen.

I had her sit beside me where I could keep an eye on her, but I was busy doing paperwork, and even in these close quarters, she was still able to cause a disturbance.

Decorations adorned the food bank and our tables were strewn with centrepieces and seasonal décor.

We had a Santa Claus greeting all the clients coming through the door and little gift bags to hand out to young ones.

It was Santa who approached me and pointed out one of our centrepieces had been vandalized.

The dove of peace had had its head cut off and its little beak was shoved up its little bum.

Santa was a little distraught, and when I asked what had happened, he nodded in Linda's direction.

I was stunned that she had managed to pull this off while sitting right beside me, and I hadn't even noticed. She didn't deny it, and when I asked her why, she told me it was to punish the person who had been short with her in the kitchen.

"But they have no idea you even did this," I pointed out.

That had no relevance. In Linda's mind, she had exacted revenge and made sure everyone knew she could not be messed with. Content and a little bored, she would suffer her penance, smug in the knowledge that she wouldn't be asked to contribute to anything else.

Linda may not have been one of the kids who felt the oneness with the community vibe I was trying to inject. I was pretty sure Santa would soldier through and the dove of peace sadly wouldn't be missed amongst the myriad of tinsel and pine cones.

Linda and her logic were a little difficult to fathom. And she wasn't done yet.

After the second day working at the food bank, we were on our way home when I decided we should stop for egg rolls as a reward for all the hard work everyone had done. Kimberly, one of the girls in the back seat, had to be nudged awake on arrival and we slowly paraded into the restaurant.

Linda immediately took off for the washroom. A waitress walking past commented on something hanging from Kimberly's coat. There, for all to see, a tampon dangled from her zipper.

Kimberly was usually easy going and a bright ray of sunshine to anyone who had the pleasure to know her. She was completely devastated and humiliated by the object hanging from her coat. She was so angry; she couldn't even speak as she quietly removed the offensive decoration.

It was obvious what had happened. Linda had asked to stop at a drug store before we went for the Chinese food, specifically to pick up some tampons she said she needed. She had always been a little resentful of Kimberly because of the attention boys paid her and because she was pretty popular all round.

Linda was still in the washroom and the girls talked about confronting her when she eventually joined us. Any semblance at trying to be friends with her had now evaporated. There had been some friction between them before but nothing exceptional. This was at a whole new level of cruelty, and it fit with Linda's way of exacting revenge for offences only she was aware of.

With all my powers of persuasion, I urged the girls not to react to what Linda had done. I was convinced that part of Linda's satisfaction would be Kimberly's reaction and seeing how she could stir up everyone else. I suggested we not talk about it at all and in this way, take away any expression of outrage.

I also thought Linda was looking for an angry reception so that she could portray herself as the victim, if that made any sense. It would fit with her constant assertions that everybody had it in for her. There should have been a backlash to what she had done, but instead, we calmly sat about and pretended nothing had happened when she got back from the bathroom.

Linda returned, sat down and looked expectantly around the table. She awaited an onslaught that never came and it obviously perturbed her. "So did anything happen?"

"What do you mean?" I responded. We weren't giving her anything to grab onto. "Did anyone find anything?" she probed.

We stared blankly in response. "Not sure what you're talking about."

She hesitated for a while. "Well, did anyone find a tampon tied to their coat?" She looked from one unresponsive face to another.

"Why would some idiot tie a tampon to their coat?" I asked.

She was immediately incensed. "Are you calling me an idiot?" Prepared to depict herself as wrongly accused, she elevated herself ever so slightly in her chair. Her indignation would have been so much more effective if she had had eyebrows.

I pretended to be confused. "No, I'm calling the person who tied the tampon to the coat an idiot."

Now it was Linda's turn to be puzzled. Did I accuse her? Indirectly I had, but she wasn't quite sure. If she continued to take offence, she was admitting to the crime.

Had we averted or merely delayed a confrontation? I know it was hard for Kimberly to find the tampon on her coat, then to have it pointed out in public by the waitress. If this had happened anywhere else without me or any other adult present, I think Linda would have had her ass kicked.

But still she still wasn't done.

Arrangements had been made for Linda to go home for Christmas. When she left our home on the 23rd, nobody really knew if she was coming back. Most of all, Linda thought she was done with us. No fond farewells.

I truly felt we had accomplished nothing with her stay. She was going home to a neurotic mother who was desperate to inject her anxieties into her daughter. She was teaching her to be apprehensive about everything and to trust no one. On top of it all, she forced her daughter to become dependent on cigarettes and reinforced any negative images Linda might have of herself.

We had Christmas with our family and a few foster kids. Most had gone home for family visits and we enjoyed a slight break.

Presents had been opened on Christmas Day and my son wanted to know what Kimberly, who had spent Christmas with us, thought of the present he had left under the tree for her. She drew a blank at his inquiry.

Thinking maybe it had got lost under the tree, we did a search, but nothing could be found. It had been a music CD and could have easily been mislaid, but something dawned on me.

"Somebody check out Linda's room," I said.

I hadn't had time to clear out her room yet, what with all the holiday preparations. Sure enough, the crumpled wrapping paper and gift tag marked to Kimberley were in her little garbage can.

I was so sad for Linda. She had done something abhorrent and I didn't think it was because she even wanted the present. I truly felt that Linda had self-esteem so low that she saw herself as someone almost impossible to love, and everything she did only confirmed this belief. She was constantly setting herself up to be the focus of negative attention.

We could easily replace Kimberly's present, but how could anyone convince Linda to stop sabotaging every relationship laid out in front of her? She did so much to hurt herself and I felt the pain of a very lonely girl intent on isolating herself. It was becoming easier to understand why she saw her spirit wolf in our field the day she arrived.

So it was with surprise and little fanfare that we found Linda being delivered back to us on the 28th of December. I tried to be sensitive to what I thought was happening, but the rest of the kids were not so enthusiastic about her presence. Enough had happened to make them distrustful of Linda and it truly was a surprise to her that she was back in our care. I don't know if her theft of the present would have happened if she knew she was coming back.

Either way, we were still in holiday spirits for the most part and I tried to keep everyone focused on the upcoming New Year. I had purchased some fireworks and, since we were so remote from neighbours, we were planning to have our own alcohol-free (of course) party.

The next few days were uneventful and the day of New Year's Eve arrived. Linda had kept to herself and the other girls were not making any friendly overtures.

It was early evening when she decided to call home to wish her family Happy New Year, and spoke to her 16-year-old sister. I was in another room when I heard Linda raising her voice. She started to cry and I could hear her begging and pleading over the phone.

"You don't have to go! Just say no!"

This went on for several minutes before she hung up. Sobbing, she told me her mother was forcing her sister into another overnight with her boyfriend's buddy, another 70-year-old looking for a 'comfort girl'.

There isn't any other way to put it. Her mother was prostituting her own daughter to keep her boyfriend happy and interested in her.

It was clear Linda's sister didn't want to go. She knew what would be expected of her and it was absolutely disgusting. I shared her heartbreak and would make sure Children's Aid knew of this forced arrangement, but otherwise was powerless.

Linda spent most of the night in her room crying and, even when she came outside for the fireworks, she displayed no joy in the explosive light show.

Screaming Eagles, Shooting Stars and sparklers reflected off her tear-stained face. The year ahead held nothing for her to celebrate.

It wasn't long into the new year that I had to take a run into town and Linda wanted to drop by an older sister's apartment to pick up something her mother had left for her—probably a carton of cigarettes. I waited outside for what turned out to be too much time, and when I went in to check, Linda was nowhere to be found. She had done a runner.

I reported it to Children's Aid immediately. There was no urgency in this event and they simply decided to return her to her mother's custody.

Less than two years later I would have an opportunity to talk to a friend of Linda's, who let me know Linda had moved in with an elderly man, yet another lonely friend of her mother's boyfriend. I know she was forced into it by her mother, who, for her own reasons, desperately clung to a man the only way she knew how.

I couldn't empathize with her. She sacrificed her children for her own security. She was a pimp, and thank God she didn't have any more daughters to distribute.

How does a woman become so desperate to hang

onto a man that she prostitutes her own daughters to his friends, just to keep him engaged?

I'm angry and sad when I think of Linda. I think from a young age she knew there was nothing to look forward to in her life, and all the different little stunts she pulled were her own cry for help.

I wish we could have made a difference, but we changed nothing in her life, and for that I'll always feel useless and incompetent. I hope her spirit wolf continues to follow her wherever she goes. I don't think there ever was anyone else looking out for her and, real or not, it gave comfort to a dark, depressing life.

I could only pray that someday she would find her way clear and maybe enjoy a normal life.

4: The newspaper caper

My home was gradually filling up as more children came to stay. These bedrooms had always been furnished, prepared for guests and visitors, and it seems they were always waiting for someone who needed the comfort they offered.

Every room had a window overlooking the scenic fields and orchards that enveloped our house. The décor was rustic and usually included quilts and fresh pillows. If space allowed, some rooms had a desk and chair in addition to a dresser and lamp.

The common areas of the house included a huge kitchen with a wood stove in the middle, expansive cupboards with appliances, a kitchen nook, a large pantry and a back room with an additional fridge under the back stairs. The dining room was also large, and I must have had a premonition of things to come when I put my hands on a long table with seating for ten bodies.

The largest windows of the house looked out over bird feeders and berry bushes that provided us red and black currants, gooseberries, raspberries and blackberries. The living room could have been larger, but still managed to squeeze in an extra-long couch, several comfy chairs and some tables, bookcases and a large TV.

It was in the living room that we received tired and often frightened children who either met us with belligerence or withdrew to hide inside a shell. Time allowed them to relax and come to terms with what was happening to them. The demands of the children varied and made them all that much more special to me as I learned about them and their histories.

Amanda was easily one of the most adorable kids to cross my threshold and, despite a sad back story, she introduced us to the resilience some kids develop in dealing with life's complications.

She was a victim of Fetal Alcohol Syndrome and this affected her physically as well as mentally. She was tall for her age of nine but clumsy with her feet and often stumbled when walking. Her skin was translucent and stretched over her thin frame, doing little to conceal the flesh and blood vessels below. She had one eye turned in and heavy bangs that formed a veil across her forehead and eyes.

Amanda seemed agreeable and complacent about being placed in a stranger's home. She had never been in care before and we would be looking after her while her mother participated in a rehab program and had some time to gather herself.

The most immediate and unfortunate issue with Amanda was that she was infested with head lice. The social worker showed me how to look for the live ones and how to strip each follicle of eggs using fingernails. She brought several bottles of medicated shampoo with her and the nit comb, but indicated the comb was not that effective.

She said I would need to dedicate hours to ridding Amanda's hair of the eggs and, with everything else I had on my plate, this was not good news. The eggs went well up the hair strands, indicating multiple in-festations and re-infestations. I had my work cut out for me.

No one shared a room in my home and I would have to keep her clothing and linens separate.

The other kids sharing our home were very pa-tient with Amanda. She struggled with things and the older kids had no trouble helping her with stuff she tried to do. A lot of them played video games in the living room and Amanda was included in this activity even though she did not have the co-ordina-tion to operate the controls. Mario Kart had a level where your figure continued to drive whether you were on track or not. The other kids would cheer Amanda on as if she was winning and she would get so excited. I was proud of the way these kids could band together and look out for each other.

I continued working on Amanda's hair and, three weeks later, things seemed to be under control. She was scheduled for a visit with her mother and was so looking forward to it. She really missed her mom during those first weeks and never stopped telling me how much she loved her.

I was glad we had a system where Amanda's mother could get help and soon be reunited with her. It always amazed me how devoted Amanda was to her mother and it was the unconditional nature of her love that kept me in awe. I struggled at times with the realization that Amanda had suffered from neglect and was permanently damaged because of her mother's addictions.

But I knew nothing of her or how her life had presented the obstacles it did. I had to remind myself that we don't always have a choice in the path laid before us.

I was however, a little disappointed when Amanda got back from her first visit. Her mother had purchased her some new shoes, but they were huge, clunky, high heeled sneakers. Amanda could barely stand upright at times, and as soon as she tried to walk across the yard, she fell. She had to hang onto the door frame just to step into our porch.

Amanda wanted to show off her new shoes, but, after congratulating her on the beautiful sneakers, I suggested she get them off and save them for special occasions. What was her mother thinking?

Then later that night, I discovered live lice on her head. They weren't there when she left and I was so discouraged to find them taking up residence once more. Back to shampooing and spending more time I didn't have trying to scrape off the eggs.

Amanda was settling in nicely and every morning, walked to the top of the driveway with the other kids to catch the bus. Our driveway entrance faced another dirt road that led to neighbours I had met when we first moved in: a retired farmer and his wife, a school teacher who admitted to not liking children. Her comment sticks with me still: "How can you stand having kids around? I don't even like my own grandchildren when they visit."

I'm sure retirement didn't come fast enough for the parents of the children she taught.

Unfortunately, while they were waiting for the bus one day, one of the kids nudged Amanda into taking the newspaper out of the neighbours' mail box. She could barely read and wasn't really up on local news so I know it wasn't her idea.

I didn't know anything about it until that evening, when both neighbours showed up at my door. I actually watched them march down the driveway with a purpose that would have impressed a Marine colonel.

I invited them in and they got right to the point. Their newspaper was gone and they were pretty sure one of my kids took it. I had both Amanda and Richard, who usually accompanied her, brought into the room and I tried to nudge the truth forward. They resisted at first but quickly reversed gears and confessed.

Not satisfied with the confirmation, my neighbours then suggested they should call the RCMP.

Things quickly deteriorated after that and I lost all patience with them. "You want to call the RCMP?" I challenged. "I've got their number right here—let me call them for you".

They were starting to back up a little at this point.

"I can't wait to hear what they have to say when I

tell them you want to report a missing newspaper!"

My teenage daughter was in the room with us and she told me later I appeared to levitate up and out of my chair. They were threatening the wrong person if they thought this was the way to set me straight.

I asked them to leave and I needed a few minutes to calm myself and decide the next course of action.

What I did next has stayed with me ever since and I don't know that I did the right thing. I wanted Amanda and Richard to know what they did was wrong. I also wanted to bring some perspective into it. It was a bloody newspaper—not the crown jewels.

Accepting responsibility was what I aimed for when I told Amanda and Richard they had to go and apologize for taking the paper. I then told them they should offer to do some work in her garden in retribution.

Looking back now, I'm not sure I should have had them do any work at all. The apology should have sufficed, but I was sensitive to any kind of backlash we might experience by having foster kids in this community. I didn't want anyone to cast a shadow on what we were doing and I desperately wanted people to know these were good, responsible children.

I don't think the kids offering to work in the garden made a difference to these people. It would take a while, but they would just bide their time and wait for the next opportunity to target my children.

We continued on doing our thing and, on one of our many trips into town, I had to stop to get gas.

This particular gas station had a large convenience shop attached and, in that store, a local dairy produ- cer had installed a fridge that made the sound of a cow mooing when you opened the door. While I was out pumping the gas, the teenagers decided to make a run just for the purpose of activating the fridge.

Amanda wasn't entirely sure what was going on but she knew she wanted to be a part of it. As she crawled out of the back seat to follow, I made a com- ment that she should be careful not to get arrested.

She hesitated briefly but her resistance was weak. She was after all, a hardened criminal after the newspaper caper. "I don't want to get arrested!" she protested as she disappeared into the store.

They were all soon back, jumping into the car as if they had just robbed a bank. They were laughing and giggling in the back seat and Amanda suggested they take another run at the fridge. I was the killjoy and insisted they wait until the next trip. I didn't want the store staff to get too irritated with us.

A few weeks later, Amanda was getting ready for another weekend visit with her mother, who was now out of rehab and back at her apartment, where Amanda was so looking forward to seeing her again. Before Amanda was ready to leave, I happened to walk into the kitchen to find her in the pantry, filling up her back pack with food.

I had a huge pantry and had it well stocked with regular groceries, home canned goods and conveni- ence items for kids' lunches. Amanda was zeroing in on puddings, crackers, juice packs and mac & cheese boxes.

Like a deer caught in the headlights, she froze while I took in what was happening. I would find this would be a common occurrence with kids who had experienced food insecurity and Amanda wouldn't be the first kid to want to take food home with them.

I told her to go ahead and take what she wanted. There was only so much she could fit in her bag and she wouldn't make a dent in what I had tucked away.

It made me sad to know that, even at her age, she knew what it was like to be hungry.

Amanda had her weekend with her mom and came back to us with more lice. This was becoming a familiar routine and we managed to keep it contained, but not without a lot of work. No one else ever became infested, but it didn't stop Amanda's mother from accusing us of being the source of the repeated outbreaks. This was irritating, but I guess she needed someone to blame.

It wasn't the only issue happening during the weekend visits.

On the way into town for a meeting with Amanda's social worker, she was talking in the back seat and I heard her telling the other kids she had watched her mother's boyfriend putting a needle in his arm and that she knew it was drugs. She didn't say her mother did it, but it was bad enough that this was taking place right in front of her. Her mother was fresh out of rehab and not allowed to be in the presence of any such activities.

I passed the information on to her social worker

for him to deal with and I felt no guilt about squealing. It was so discouraging to know what some of these kids had to endure when they needed to be protected and nurtured. I didn't have a good image of Amanda's mother.

With bad impressions instilled in my mind, it was that much more awkward when, on our next visit to social services, Amanda's worker told me her mother was in the next room and wanted to meet me. My protests fell on deaf ears.

This woman had probably had a horrible life, but I still struggled to emphasize with her when I knew how much Amanda now and forever would suffer. Fetal Alcohol Syndrome had left her so damaged; she would never be like other kids and would endure a life that would not always be a kind or safe place for her to live in.

I entered the room and Amanda's mother stood up and immediately clasped my hand, shaking it vigorously. She was a large and very tall women with short black hair and I could see the resemblance to Amanda. She thanked me again and again for looking after her daughter, and I found myself stumbling over words that complimented her on what a wonderful child she had.

I tried to avoid any pitfalls like mentioning some of Amanda's problems. Instead, I smiled and desperately tried to keep things pleasant and casual.

This wouldn't be the last time I would be thrown into the clutches of a parent eager to connect with the surrogate parents Children's Aid provided. I might eventually come to terms with it, but it was al-ways a situation I forced myself to push through.

We returned home to the wintry delight of soft snow falling.

The white blanket thickened overnight and we woke up to the sound of a snow mobile tearing it up in the fields surrounding our house. The driver was enjoying the open fields but he also was having a great time buzzing through the little hollow that sep-arated the house from the poultry barns. I don't know what the speed was, but the machine was at full throttle as he made several passes not more than 30 yards from my house.

Then I got a phone call from the RCMP about "our" irresponsible behaviour with "our" snow-mo-bile and how it was terrorizing the neighbours. It didn't seem to have a lot of impact when I tried to explain we didn't have a snowmobile or anyone who even knew how to drive one. The officer was persist-ent in questioning me on my 17-year-old son who only visited part time, and how he could easily be the one responsible for the disruption.

Again, I explained we didn't have a snowmobile and I suggested he come out to the farm and follow the tracks. Whoever it was, was also a threat to my cats and if the kids had been out playing, a danger to them as well.

Over the next few weeks, I would receive more calls from the police as a result of neighbours blam-ing my son for violating their private property on a black Polaris. I didn't need to think too hard about who was making the complaints. There was a hint of desperation our neighbours' attempts to find something on the children in my home.

This was such a contrast to so many others in the community who welcomed us, and was not at all reflective of the way people looked at foster children. This wasn't mentioned in any of the training we had received but it was something we would learn to deal with and do our best to insulate our kids from.

Easter arrived and I had a full house for dinner that Sunday. I had a large table in the dining room and I had to set up an additional table to accommodate the overflow. On these special occasions, I always brought out the family china, silverware and crystal glasses.

Among the guests at our table that day were friends who brought with them their teenage son. I can remember a comment the mother made about the table I'd set, and how she would never use expensive dinnerware with children.

I was of a completely different philosophy. These were dishes and silver that had been in my family for almost two centuries and the crystal I had collected on my own. I felt they were made to be used, not just to decorate a china cabinet. I put them to use each Christmas, New Years, Thanksgiving and Easter, and had never lost a piece yet.

With the meal over and my friends' comments still ringing in my ears, I remember looking around the dining room after almost everyone had left. Amanda was still sitting at the kid's table. She was looking off in the distance, her legs casually crossed and a wine glass delicately balanced in her hands.

I don't know what her daydream was, but she looked so content, and very comfortable with the elegant dinnerware. At peace with the world, she looked quite natural holding the fragile crystal, and I didn't regret for one second letting the kids eat off my family heirlooms.

I'm pretty sure my ancestors would have approved everything still finding purpose so many years later. These were special occasions and I wanted everyone to feel a part of the experience in its entirety.

Not long after Easter, I began to think about excursions for the kids that could be interesting but possibly a little expensive. I approached some of the social workers about a day trip to Moncton, a couple of hours away from us, so that the children could experience Crystal Palace indoor fun park. They advised me to try writing a proposal with cost estimates and to submit it to the head of Children Services. I had no idea if this was something that had ever been done before, but nothing ventured, nothing gained.

The response was almost immediate and I received approval to make a special outing for us all. I quickly set to work setting things in motion and I was glad I had been thorough in the budget I had detailed.

Our special day arrived and I had four children with me—two teenagers and a nine- and a ten-year-old. Amanda was thrilled to be a part of this excursion and even the teens couldn't contain their excitement.

It was a long drive but we got there mid-morning and the kids set to work checking out all the rides and attractions available. I had also included in the budget submission some spending money, so I handed their portion over to the teens and hung onto the cash for the younger ones.

Rides were the biggest interest and after a couple of hours standing in line ups, I was happy the teens took over watching the younger ones while I sat on a bench within sight of everyone.

Lunch came and they begged for the carnival food while I pressed for a well-known family restaurant nearby. I lost and they very much enjoyed their junk food.

There were a couple more hours of wandering the park, and eventually everyone found a little jewellery kiosk. The girls were drawn to some pretty butterfly rings. It was decided that they would form a butterfly club, with membership restricted to only those who participated in this odyssey. The one boy in the group chose a butterfly bracelet and they all gifted me a little necklace to commemorate the trip.

I was touched at this gesture and so grateful that we had such an amazing day.

There was a movie theatre in the complex and I managed to persuade them to take in a recently-released show and let my sore feet have a rest. They were starting to tire out and I had little resistance when I tried again to persuade them to take supper at the family restaurant across the park. It was in the budget that had been approved and I didn't want to let the opportunity for a good meal go to waste. The energy level had definitely subsided and even eating seemed like hard work.

We soon set off home and it was less than fifteen minutes before everyone fell asleep.

I considered the expedition a success. They had had a great day and were totally exhausted as a result. They had won prizes, bought themselves treats and proudly displayed on the fingers of three hands were the beautiful little butterfly rings. Children's Aid had made this day possible and I, for one, was honoured to be wearing their symbol of the sorority around my neck.

Eventually, Amanda's time with us came to an end and she was released back to her mother's custody. Many years later, I was at a local high school, participating in a health fair, when I recognized Amanda approaching my booth. She did not recognize me and I did not identify myself, as it was part of Children's Aid's rules that kids no longer in care not be bothered by their previous foster parents.

She was so tall and thin and I almost didn't realize who she was. She was quietly curious and went through the displays alone, smiling occasionally when something tweaked her interest. She was still wrapped in a fragile blanket of innocence and I wanted so much to believe she was in a good place, with both herself and her mom doing well.

I had no idea if Children's Aid was still involved in her life. That would have depended on how successful her mother had been in dealing with her own struggles.

I still had the urge to want to protect her, but I had no right to concern myself in her life. I crossed my fingers and prayed for the best, but never saw or heard any more about her.

I think the hardest thing about being a foster parent is getting involved with a child but never having any follow-up to wherever their life might lead them, good or bad. Without any entitlement, we are left to wonder about their fate and can do nothing more than wish them the best on their journey.

5: Politics and a free lunch

Richard came to us in the early spring, a small boy of 11 who brought with him his own challenges. He was friendly, sociable and eager to fit in with this strange new environment.

Richard's situation was a sad story, with a father who had passed away from cancer a few years earlier. They had been such a big part of each other's lives, and then his mother had decided to move on and remarry.

The new family unit included a new little sister and somehow, Richard's mother could not cope with his behaviour. He did have some behavioural issues, but I didn't think he had anything that serious.

His social worker told me that Richard had mild Tourette's, which expressed itself in constant squinting and the need to hop around a lot. He had also been diagnosed with ADHD which would require attention, but so many of the children coming through our door carried this or other issues with them that it had become the norm.

Richard was to have visits with his grandmother on some weekends; no overnights, just a quick couple of hours. I knew nothing else about the situation and again found myself trying not to judge why his mother had put him in care.

Richard was eager to involve himself with anything and everything we had going on, and one of our latest interests had been the incubation of eggs. We had several duck eggs and a couple of peacock eggs to work on and each kid, if they chose, would be the owner of an egg. We would all take turns being responsible for monitoring temperature, humidity and making sure they were all turned at the same time.

A friend had lent me a small incubator with a window on top and we marked each egg with a number so everyone knew which one was their egg. One of the conditions of participating was that, somewhere down the line, you would have a duck that would have to leave with you or that would have to be eaten. In the meantime, they would be your pet to look after until they joined the other ducks in the poultry barn.

I wasn't expecting kids to show up for family visits with a duck in tow, but the point had to be made that this was a farm and most of our birds were destined for the dinner table—it was a fact of life the kids needed to deal with.

I had recently had a sad situation in which a child came to me from another foster home where, just before they left, they had been given a puppy from a litter there. This wasn't fair to us, as we had two cats and ducks and guineas that roamed free now that spring was well in gear.

I had to say no, and I was more than a little miffed that these people would do this with no consideration for our home or what bringing a puppy into it would entail. I wasn't ready to take on the responsibility and it made me out to be the bad guy as a result.

The incubator was in our dining room and a clipboard showed whose shift it was each day to look after the eggs and report any news. I can't remember how many days the eggs took, but all of the duck eggs hatched successfully while the peacocks did not.

Four or five kids participated, and we had a box set up for nursing the little ones with their proper feed and water, as well as a heat lamp. There were patchy markings on the ducks that were immediately evident on hatching, and some of the kids were able to witness their own duck come into the world as it broke through the shell.

It was a slow process and some took a couple of hours to complete their emergence, but it was so exciting for the kids to see.

Everyone quickly named their duck, and they were allowed to sit and watch TV holding their duckling on a bed of clean rags in their lap. It was a peaceful scene, with the little yellow bundles dotting the living room on several laps.

One of the teenagers took an opportunity to pull a trick on me with the name they chose for their ward. They called their duck 'Corn olio'. It wasn't until several weeks later, when the head of the foster parents' alliance visited me, that I found out I'd been had.

We were sitting out on my porch and she asked me if I knew where the name came from. I told her I assumed it was a cartoon character like something from Sponge-Bob. Keeping a straight face, she told me what cornholing actually meant.

I had been going around, talking to people about the ducklings for over two weeks and sharing all the names. No one stepped forward to enlighten me. Maybe they thought I was in on it and didn't have a problem with the name. I did, but I have to say, as far as jokes go, they got me good.

As part of my ongoing efforts to involve the children in local activities, I decided we should attend the opening of a new public beach close to our farm. Attached to the beach and extending out on an isthmus of land would also be serviced building lots for sale by a local developer.

I let everyone know what we were doing. It was a Saturday morning, so not everyone had a lot of enthusiasm for the outing. Richard was keen to go, as were a few other of the younger ones, but we were missing the teenagers.

We arrived and made our way down to the beach area, where a lot of adults were milling about. A great billboard had been erected at the end of the beach, with a map outlining all the lots and marking the ones which had already been sold.

There were some local politicians, some community leaders and a few members of the media. An area had been set up with a microphone and different people took turns making their speeches about community access and the housing development making good business for us all. My kids were politely quiet but not attentive to what was coming across the sound system.

They became little more interested, however, when journalists decided they wanted to hear the perspective of young people. Some reporters held microphones while others just took notes, but they paid close attention to the responses from my kids, who basked in the attention they were getting.

We were then invited over to a nearby community hall in an old, converted school house, where a local women's auxiliary had laid out an amazing buffet. It was now the turn of the politicians to seek out the opinion of my children and I think they did quite well.

I can remember watching Richard from a distance as he kept hitching up his pants while he talked to a provincial MLA. Richard often would shove his fists deep into his pant pockets, pushing the waistband down till it got to the point where he was almost indecent. When the pants needed to be pulled up, he could twist the waistband back and forth without removing his hands from his pockets and, like magic, the waistband eventually worked its way upwards. It was an unconscious thing and for some reason, punctuated his youth and innocence as he shared his thoughts.

All of the kids loved being asked what they thought about the whole project, and I suddenly realized I had brought the only children present and almost everyone wanted to talk to them.

When Richard wasn't being interviewed, he was filling up plates of sandwiches and squares and kept showing me his loot like a pirate filling up his chest. I suggested to him that we take back some of the sweets for the kids at home and he was blunt with his response: "If they wanted some of this food, they should have come and got some themselves. I'm not taking them anything!"

I think the organizers had overestimated the attendance and the ladies were happy to help load up my kids for our trip home. Richard kept his word and refused to share, continuing to lecture the others on the early bird catching the worm and so forth.

I decided then that I wouldn't miss any openings involving politicians. They had great catering and the interest they displayed toward young people made it worthwhile.

Telling people about it being one of our favourite activities would always be met with strange looks. For anyone presenting a challenge to our unusual recreational obsession, I could always refer them to Richard. He could set them straight if you weren't distracted by the iced brownies smeared around his lips.

As congenial as Richard was, life was not without controversy in our home. He was oppositional and never stopped trying to find new ways to disobey our house rules. One of the most contentious issues was the requirement that everyone keep their room clean. He continually failed inspection, mainly because he refused to pick up his dirty clothes. I would find them hidden behind his bed, tucked behind his door, anywhere but in the dirty laundry, and the effort he put into not co-operating was so much more than if he had just done it in the first place.

On top of that, each time he lied to me about doing his work, he would be consequenced, but it would never discourage him from doing it again and again. So, things could get unpleasant between us and I know he was getting pretty frustrated.

I remembered hearing something about when married couples experienced troubles and how, no matter what transpired through the day, they would try never to go to bed angry. Stewing over things said and unsatisfied arguments wasn't healthy to dwell on through the night and I compared this to the continuous disagreements Richard and I had every single day.

I decided that, before it was time for him to go to bed at night, we would go out on the porch, have a cup of tea together, and tell jokes. It would only be ten or fifteen minutes, but it would be time to decompress and make peace. This worked for us both because I could be angry about the latest stunt he had pulled and he was always losing privileges.

This was to become the highlight of every day for us both. He so enjoyed sitting there and we never missed a night once the practice started.

Sometimes other kids would have their faces pressed up against the kitchen window, wanting to come out and join us. I always left this up to Richard.

This was our time, and periodically he would let others come out, but for the most part he wanted this quiet time for just the two of us.

Years later, I would hear from others who knew him and he told many people about how much he enjoyed it, except that he didn't like tea!

As sociable and easy-going as Richard was, he seemed to have a lot of anxiety about people drinking alcohol. We always had a few bottles of hard liquor on hand for personal use or for guests, but weren't in the habit of drinking on a regular basis.

One day at the store, I found some Perrier water in tall green cans instead of the usual bottles and I bought them as a treat for myself. This really bothered Richard; he was convinced they were some form of beer. Several times I showed him the label, but it worried him so much, I had to tuck them away and forego the pleasure until some day when he would not be with us.

Then we decided to have a party for a friend's 40th birthday and we were planning to have wine and beer. Richard again started to agitate about what was going to happen, and when I asked him why it was such a big deal, he told me he didn't like it when the fist fights broke out.

I've had gatherings for years and haven't had an altercation yet. I don't really know what Richard had been exposed to, but apparently it was standard to have things get physical at the parties he had seen.

I tried to assure him that it wasn't the usual practice and I didn't hide the fact that the adults might get loud, but said they certainly wouldn't be hitting each other. We also would be limiting how much alcohol we served because we needed to make sure people could safely drive home. There would also be designated drivers who didn't partake at all.

I hoped we showed the kids a responsible way to behave when consuming alcohol, and Richard did start to relax a bit.

One of my responsibilities in looking after the children was making sure their clothing allowance was spent wisely. I would go into town to do shopping for all the kids. This was an outing for everyone and we would hit the mall in town, check out several stores and, with luck, enjoy some success in finding what was needed.

Once the business part was taken care of, I would let teens have some time hanging around the food court and, although Richard was only 11, I allowed him go along. This was a privilege for him and the others did agree to watch over him.

The first time I did this, I left everyone to get themselves a treat and I wandered down the mall to do some shopping of my own. Within five minutes, one of the teens angrily brought Richard to me and, through clenched teeth, told me he could not be left with them.

Apparently, he had grabbed a cigarette off an ashtray on someone's table, took a puff and returned it to the ashtray. Reaction was immediate from the person who owned the cigarette and the teens were quickly targeted with looks from many pinched, disapproving faces.

Richard was quite nonchalant about the whole thing and, despite having no explanation for his actions, didn't seem to understand what the whole fuss was about. I decided the consequence would be that he would have to spend the rest of the shopping trip at my side, no matter where I went or what I did.

I considered it a punishment—Richard did not. He was chatty the entire time and seemed quite at peace with the whole thing. He even tried to offer his ADHD as an explanation for grabbing the cigarette.

I did not accept this. I understood his behaviour might be challenged by it, but having ADHD didn't mean he had lost all control of his actions or was not still responsible for what he did.

Richard wasn't the first kid in my care to tell me what they did wasn't their fault because of ADD, ADHD, etc. I envisioned counsellors in our community giving them an out for their unacceptable behaviour. I felt then, and still do feel, that children with behavioural disorders don't need excuses. What they need is coping mechanisms—ways of recognizing when something is happening and being able to take a hold of it before something serious takes place. Richard thought he had a blank cheque for his conduct, and I cancelled it.

Despite his odd behaviour on the trip to the mall, I persuaded the teens to take charge of Richard on the next trip to town. Same deal as before, where he could spend time just hanging around the food court, grab a snack and relax...but he did it again.

This was final for the teens. They delivered Richard to me after he had grabbed french fries from someone's plate in the food court and casually munched them as if he didn't have a care in the world.

I told him he would never be allowed to hang out with the older kids again. There was no reaction or protest from Richard, and he didn't deny grabbing the fries. When I told him he would now and forever be glued to me every time we went anywhere, he just squinted.

Then I noticed how relaxed and at ease he was. He had just created a scene which took away what I thought was a privilege, but was it?

Richard was happy to follow me around, talking nonsense and making conversation about anything and everything. It was almost as if he had pulled these stunts for the purpose of being made to stay with me and not with the other kids.

It took a while to sink in, but I don't think Richard was comfortable hanging around the mall. The teens he could have been spending time with were kids he got along with fine at home, so it wasn't them. Was he looking for the security of an adult?

Looking back now, I realize how some kids might be desperate to fill in the gap left by a missing parent. His father had passed away and his mother had put him in foster care. For better or worse, maybe I was filling a hole in his life and it wasn't because I was special. He was clinging to me like someone would cling to a life preserver after the ship has gone down.

I didn't know the psychology of it, but it did seem that he would sabotage any outing with other youth simply because they didn't offer what he was looking for.

So now I had to implement a policy that, anytime we went anywhere, Richard would be at my side, and this would prevent any other fiascoes, right? Wrong!

A few weeks later, we were grocery shopping and it was a warm day, so I bought Richard a cold soda that he could have once we got out to the car to load up bags. While we were in the store, someone had pulled up beside our car in one of those beautiful, vintage classic cars. Lovingly restored, painted and waxed, it was a work of art.

As I paused to admire the car, I failed to notice Richard shaking his can of soda. As soon as he flipped the top, it sprayed the antique car like an out-of-control fire hose. It was an open top car, so when the cream soda came shooting out of the can, it not only got the side of the car, it peppered the lovely leather interior as well!

Richard didn't spray the car on purpose, but shaking the can had a predictable result.

My first instinct was to run. My second was to see if there were any witnesses. No one appeared to have noticed what had happened, but I truly did not want to hang around and meet the car's owner. This was a treasure to whomever had put so much love and devotion into it.

We had to do something so, after giving Richard a quick dressing down, I had him run into the store and get some damp paper towels. I was afraid to use soap of any kind and I had no idea what the ingredients of the soda might do to the finish of the car.

I had Richard gently dab at the legion of droplets on the body of the car, but could not let him climb into the car to clean the leather.

The right thing to do would have been to wait around for the owner. But I was genuinely scared. I had no idea what their temperament would have been, but I couldn't handle someone yelling at me and I was the person ultimately responsible for what had happened.

I should have been paying more attention to Richard. He was just doing something dumb when he shook the can and I don't think he even noticed the car when he let loose the spray. Never a dull moment.

We drove away without leaving any confessions.

For every negative there is a positive, and so too were my feelings about Richard. He was an enigma to me and I often found myself marvelling at things he did and the way he acted.

I noticed he liked to be around men, no matter the occasion. One day we stopped to get some air put in a tire and, as Wade got out to talk to a garage employee, Richard hopped out like a flash and stood beside the guys as they chatted man talk. Richard would occasionally contribute, but I noticed that when he listened to someone, instead of tilting his whole head up, he would instead lean his body backwards as if he were fighting a stiff breeze.

He didn't miss these opportunities, no matter if it was a pit stop for soft drinks or a trip to the hardware store. The same was true at auctions, where farmers formed groups to exchange opinions. Richard didn't know a thing about farming but he was eager to melt into discussions on any range of topics if men were doing the talking.

While Richard stayed with us full time, he did have occasional weekend visits with his grandmother. These were not an overnight but a couple of hours on a Saturday or Sunday afternoon. An aid would come out to pick him up and, although the visits were not supervised, they would always be close at hand.

The grandmother had a boyfriend, and during Richard's visits the boyfriend would pick on him and make fun of him, calling him a spoiled brat and so forth.

I don't know why the boyfriend had to be there during those visits, but, one afternoon, Richard had had enough and lit out from his grandmother's house. The aid was hot on his heels but could not get close enough to him, despite begging him to stop and come back to their car.

She called me and frantically described the situation and that they were now walking, sometimes running, through the woods of a nearby park.

I don't think I'm very original on my own but I have no trouble borrowing ideas from others. I had read an account of a mom who couldn't get her kids to help tidy the house and she started crying out 'the queen is coming, the queen is coming—we need to get the house cleaned up!' and with that they all pitched in before they realized they had been tricked.

On the spot, I decided to try something similar and asked if the aid could get Richard to take the phone because I urgently needed to talk to him.

He allowed her to get near enough to pass the phone over and I pleaded with him. "The ducks are out and I can't get them in and the fox is going to get them!"

He immediately turned around, handed back the phone, and headed to the aid's car. I had told him I needed him and instantly he was ready to come home.

I think he was also tired of the whole business of being teased, and why his grandmother allowed her boyfriend to ruin their visit, I'll never know.

The truth was I actually *did* need him back to help me with the ducks. Richard came back, helped me get the ducks in and I was very grateful he chose to be there for me when I genuinely needed him. I thought it was very gallant of him to come to my rescue, and I let him know how appreciative I was.

There would be other visits with his grandmother and the boyfriend continued to be a presence that made the excursions unpleasant. Often, after an unsuccessful trip, I would receive hang-up calls and I eventually had them traced to his grandmother.

There wouldn't have been a problem with letting her talk to Richard, but if he wasn't the one answering the phone, she would drop the receiver.

I eventually had to ask his social worker to intervene and put a stop to it. The worker followed up with me and told me his grandmother was a confused, sweet old lady.

That isn't the way I would reflect on it.

Another activity we participated in as a group was attending estate auctions. These were generally old farms, some of which were sadly packing it in, and everything had to go.

I would pack a picnic lunch, take a couple of blankets and, when we arrived, I would register for our bidding number. I gave each kid no more than five dollars, and they would wander around to see what treasures there might be had amongst all the dusty old boxes and farm equipment. Once the auction started, we would wave our number when the price was right, and see just how much five dollars could get you.

Box lots were the cheapest things because they were boxes that anything and everything had been thrown into. My kids bid on and won a box with old used drinking glasses, not because we were going to use the glasses but because hidden in the box was a big jar of old marbles.

Another kid bought me a bed—an old, cast-iron bed that had been painted so many times and it only cost two dollars! It went directly into the carriage shed as a future project, but what a deal.

I would find picture frames and old cookie tins. One kid bought the most interesting-looking set of oil cans made of copper and pretty greasy, but if someone wanted to clean them up, they could have made some money.

It was another means of entertainment and they found it exciting to wave our card and hear the hammer come down when a sale was made.

The baby ducks matured and were put out with the adults. Everyone still knew which one was their duck and they were very tame, coming when they were called and always up for a snuggle.

Then decision time came, when they were big enough to put away in the freezer or, if arrangements could be made, sent to live somewhere else.

Richard struggled with knowing his duck was destined for the dinner table, but he did come to terms with it. This was a poultry farm, and it was a fact of life that we were not vegetarians and included a wide range of meat at our table.

I knew a local gentleman who professionally smoked and sold quite a bit of meat, and he had looked after turkeys for us the year before. This year I decided to have some of the ducks smoked as well, and Richard's was one of them. The Muscovy duck is like a cross between a turkey and a duck and has a large meat breast and is not so greasy as a regular duck.

Richard's duck was smoked and we had it for our Sunday dinner late that summer. I remember when we all sat down to the table, Richard had a long face and made the comment, "I don't know if I can eat a friend."

I was feeling guilty to some degree, but a little less so when I realized that Richard was reaching for a second helping of smoked duck.

It didn't end there. He ate the meat like he was ravenous and was actually quite proud that he had raised the bird that graced our table. And it was amazing! It didn't taste like a turkey, but it was a large bird and there weren't any leftovers.

Richard wasn't the only one who appreciated the unique flavour and I was glad I had five more in the freezer for our own personal use.

Richard shared so many memories with us and other children in our home. He was there with us when we made our excursion to Crystal Palace in New Brunswick and joined us in our butterfly club. He was the child who egged Amanda into taking the newspaper out of our neighbour's mailbox and regrettably did some gardening for them.

It took a while, but Children's Aid did find a wonderful permanent foster home for him, and I knew Richard was going to enjoy all the love and attention he deserved from a caring, supportive family.

I was happy to see him move on, and thinking of him still brings a smile to my face.

6: The kingdom of teachers' aides

Kevin came to us a frail, gangly boy of 13, a long-term guest of Children's Aid. He was a permanent member of a system designed to protect and nourish him, and he was yet another child I was privileged to meet and welcome into my home.

He brought with him a necessity for close attention, medical needs requiring regular prescription monitoring and behaviour sometimes out of his control. Kevin had Tourette's along with ADHD and neither of them in a small measure.

Medication controlled the Tourette's for the most part, except first thing in the morning, when there was a response period of about 20 to 30 minutes. It was for this reason we decided to place him in a downstairs bedroom, where he would be apart from the others and less likely to disturb anyone while we waited for the pills to kick in. He would be barking and yelping as he dressed and did his washroom routine.

Then ADHD handicapped him from completing any task without losing track of where he was or what he was supposed to be doing. Nothing was fluid for Kevin, and simple tasks like packing his school bag found him flitting off like a butterfly in so many directions each time something distracted him.

He had been assigned a dedicated teacher's aide who had the additional responsibility of picking him up in the morning from our home and delivering him back to us at the end of the school day. Kevin couldn't have been left to get on and off a bus on his own.

Time spent together meant a long day for them both, and starting off seemed to be the worst part. She would arrive around 7:30 and would start going through a checklist of what Kevin needed to have with him. I would be in the kitchen making lunches and it could take 10-15 minutes before Kevin actually had everything packed and his shoes on, ready to go out the door—so I thought. Then she would start in on whether he had put on enough deodorant.

This was the point I really started to dislike her. While Kevin was hovering around doing his thing, she would comment to me about his body odour and couldn't I smell it? She was stuck in the car with him for the 40-minute drive to school and apparently struggled to breathe for some of the trips. Didn't he ever shower at our place?

I hadn't noticed a thing, and showering was a part of his regular hygiene.

What really irritated me was how she talked about this in front of Kevin as if he wasn't there. Her face would be all twisted up as she curled her nose and went on at length about the issue.

This definitely would have been my responsibility, and I took it seriously; but, try as I might, Kevin didn't present the offensive odour to me that it did to her. His room was off the dining room and if he was as pungent as the aide insisted he was, I would have thought we might have noticed something escaping his bedroom.

Kevin seemed to ignore her barrage of complaints, but I wondered if the negative remarks were accumulating somewhere in his psyche.

Eventually, I suggested she just wait in her car and let me help him get organized. I didn't do it any better than she did, but I did do it without the ceaseless condescending remarks about his lack of body care. He was constantly moving and it wouldn't have been a shocker that he suffered from excessive sweating, but I was confident I sent him off with his hygiene under control.

By the time Kevin would be returned to me in the evening, he had amassed so much pent-up energy in his thin body, he was like a rubber band that's been wound too tight. He would literally run on tip toes from one end of the house to the other and it was a challenge just to keep out of his way.

The teacher's aide always came into the house and often had a list of instructions for me on what Kevin had to accomplish during the evening.

This particular night, I had one of my kids attending a Taekwondo class in town later on and I beamed at Kevin when I told him the rest of us were all going swimming during the interval.

She couldn't have been snottier when she told me I would have to make other arrangements with the other children because Kevin had at least two more hours of homework to do and certainly wasn't available to join us.

Children's Aid had entrusted me with quite a few kids, and I felt it was part of my job to keep them happy and healthy. Physical activities and having fun were a big part of what I included in their schedules and Kevin wasn't going to be excluded from them.

The teacher's aid was an absolute horror of a human being, demanding Kevin not be permitted to participate in our activities. I ignored the instructions to monitor the additional assignments.

While Kevin was in my home, I was responsible for him and he needed an outlet for all that energy he had been forced to contain. She didn't even let him out in the school yard after he had his lunch.

We went to town and had a great swim, picked up my Taekwondo student and back we came. The drive home was always a lot quieter than the one into town and it satisfied me that everyone was tired out.

The next morning, I went out with Kevin when he was getting into the aide's car and let her know I had declined her invitation to supervise the homework she had assigned.

She was livid! Speechless, she angrily put her car in gear and off they went.

This was not over, and I couldn't help feeling she

might take her frustrations out on Kevin.

Later that morning, I got a call from the head of Children's Services, asking me to attend a meeting that afternoon in town with Kevin's social worker, herself and the teacher's aide. Apparently, she did not go quietly into the night.

Conflict is never something I was afraid to engage in, and I happily made the journey, not sure what to expect but confident the proverbial s--t had hit the fan.

Seating is always a telling tool in any meeting, and I found myself facing the teachers aide, who sat beside the head supervisor while Kevin's social worker and I sat opposite.

We were asked to detail what had happened the night before and the teacher's aide accurately provided her side, along with the demands she made for Kevin's homework and my obvious refusal.

I reinforced the same version except I added one grenade: "I don't take orders from a teacher's aide."

At this statement her entire neck and face flushed a brilliant red.

I went on to describe how Kevin was always delivered to me with such pent-up energy he literally burst through the door each evening. Forcing him to sit still for an additional two hours was pure torture and I wasn't going to do it. He spent ten hours of each day with that woman and I don't want to dismiss how hard it was for her to get him to focus on his work, but there had to be limits.

I was questioned on how Kevin acted in our home

and what activities I included the kids in. I had managed to secure discounted memberships to several places in our area which included the swimming pool of a local hotel, purchased memberships for a local paintball enterprise and time at the gymnasium of a nearby university. I also organized weekend excursions to historic sites and walking trails, and took advantage of any festival or fairs laid on in nearby communities. I even made them go to art exhibits.

I kept the kids busy and the results spoke for themselves. Children with behavioural issues were enjoying some success at my home and I think it had something to do with the relaxation, the farm activities, the respect I tried to give them and keeping them busy with healthy activities.

I was thanked for the information I had provided and told they would be in touch.

They weren't. I didn't hear anything more from Children's Aid on the subject and, without direction one way or the other, I kept right on doing what I was doing. I assumed the aide had been told to back off.

Communication continued to be difficult with the teacher's aide, but battle lines had been drawn. Occasionally, if time permitted, I would help Kevin with some homework, but my focus would remain on helping the kids relax and have fun.

It was that time of year for a local military base to have its annual Armed Forces Day, and I loaded up the car with my husband, my teenage son and three foster children including Kevin. I say local, but it was actually well over an hour away in Shearwater, and I thought it would be of interest to Kevin especially. It was always a big production, with so many displays and exhibits as well as the air show that never failed to excite and amaze us.

It never occurred to me that such close contact and opportunity to touch and feel so many things might over-stimulate him. Kevin became intoxicated by the close-up and hands-on instrument panels, weapons displays and tours of large personal carriers and helicopters.

I realized there was a problem when I found myself constantly calling out, "Where's Kevin?"

Trying to keep up with him was like trying to chase an Indian rubber ball—once let loose it just kept going. What he hadn't yet seen became an emergency. What he had already seen needed a second, third and maybe even fourth tour.

We had a particularly hard time trying to keep him still out on the tarmac while we waited for the air show. Our constant chorus of 'Where's Kevin?' continued throughout the afternoon with my husband and teenage son frequently sent to hunt him down. He was absorbing so much and I thought he was going to erupt from the sights and sounds he was digesting.

I found myself wondering if Kevin had the ability to someday be a pilot or navigator. Why not? He was a smart kid and, if things could settle down for him, it was a possibility I encouraged him to consider.

While others fell asleep on the drive home, Kevin

was still wired and eager to talk about what he had seen and done that day. I was glad we had the opportunity to let him check out what Canada's military had to offer. I think he would have enlisted that day if they were looking for hyperactive 13-year-olds.

It was excursions like this I was happy to organize for anyone I had staying with me. We enjoyed them as a family and I was happy to share these experiences with the kids in my care.

Another aspect of trotting around the province was having to constantly figure out how to feed any number of kids. Sometimes getting someone to a class or activity in the evening meant I didn't have time to lay out a supper. If we had spent a weekend day out and were coming home late, we were all too tired to fix a meal when returning home.

One of our activities was to go bowling, and the alley we frequently used had a score sheet that included on it a coupon for an international sub shop —buy one six inch get one free. I used these coupons every chance I could as something convenient and what I thought was a decent option for fast food.

One evening after a couple of rounds of bowling, I approached the young man at the counter and asked about the unused coupons on a stack of score sheets left by other bowlers. Would he mind if I grabbed a couple of the sandwich coupons? What he did next amazed me. He started organizing the sheets and went to work with scissors. By the time he was done and I had a chance to count, he let me have 97 coupons!

This was a Godsend to me. I could feed a lot of kids a snack or temporary meal with these coupons and I couldn't thank him enough.

As he handed them to me, he said, "Happy Mother's Day!"

I could have kissed him!

Our home was getting busier with foster children and it was inevitable that one of them would show up with head lice (Amanda). She was well engaged with the little creatures and we immediately began the process of shampoos and combing. Unfortunately, every time she went home for a visit, she came back re-infested. I'm sure you've heard the expression 'Revenge is a dish best served cold'. I was about to experience a backlash to my previous battle with Kevin's teacher's aide.

When she found out someone in my house had lice, it was her opportunity to go on the offensive. She literally skipped gleefully up to my door and started in on how she couldn't have someone in her car with lice and her husband used the vehicle to attend business meetings and he can't conduct himself professionally if he's scratching himself, and it went on and on.

Kevin never had lice and actually no one else in our house ever contracted them, but this was of no relevance. It was her chance to give me a hard time after she had been knocked off her pedestal about the control of Kevin's nighttime activities.

It was weeks before the situation was under control and I can't say how many lectures I was forced to endure. And as hard a time as she was giving me, I know she was also laying into Kevin, who had no control over the situation whatsoever.

This lady had a professional responsibility to treat Kevin with respect, but kindness was definitely not something I ever saw her extend to him. It was such a contrast to the wonderful work I saw other teachers engaged in when dealing with my kids. The unscheduled nature of having foster kids dropping into classrooms wasn't always easy for them to accommodate, but it was never something they would have passed on to the kids.

This teacher's aide was missing any semblance of care and consideration for Kevin, and her true sentiments towards him were flagrantly on display in my home. She had to obscure her treatment of him anywhere else but our place. How could anyone listen to the way she spoke to him and not report her? Children's Aid already knew what I thought of her. I kept hoping they would never use her again to work with one of their wards—she simply didn't have what it took.

Spring was melting into summer and it was during this time that I had family visit from out west. My brother, his wife and my four-year-old nephew joined us for just over a week, and it was nice to have their company.

Unfortunately, my nephew was curious and, while exploring the house, wandered into Kevin's room and touched some of his things while he was off at school.

111

Kathleen Foster-Alfred

Kevin was furious when he got home, and I understood his concerns. How seriously he took this inva-
sion of his privacy was not immediately apparent. I
didn't realize he felt his privacy had been violated
and would respond in a most inappropriate way.

The next morning, I woke and went down to get
Kevin up, only to find him wide awake and all the
lights downstairs turned on. A spider web of string
was affixed around his door and inside I could see
sections of paper towel covering his floor.

When I asked him why he had littered his floor he
told me he needed to hide the surprise he had in
store for "that little bastard". There was nothing
playful in his tone.

I removed the string and pulled up some of the
paper to find broken glass distributed over his bedroom floor. It was heartbreaking to find the elabor-
ate trap Kevin had set up for my nephew. And I felt
partially responsible because my nephew should
never have been in Kevin's room in the first place.

This was an extreme reaction to a minor problem
and I had no choice but to report it to his social
worker. I had concerns about the safety of my family
and I worried about this turn of events. I was pretty
sure Kevin had never done anything like this before
and he may have felt provoked, but his reaction was
way out of line. I wasn't sure if the string was intended to deter my nephew from getting in or if it was
supposed to strangle him. To lay shards of broken
glass all over the floor and then conceal them was
malicious and calculating.

This is what bothered me the most—Kevin had never shown any signs of wanting to hurt anyone before. Why now? We had also toured the military base on Armed Forces Day—did that have any influence in his reaction? Did he think he had to defend his room with force? What motivated him to respond the way he did?

I didn't know anything about his early life, and maybe there were clues to be found there.

A few days later, Kevin was removed from our home. I had never asked for him to be removed and I was truly sad to see him go. I thought he was a fantastic young man who had some kinks that needed to be worked out, but he still had so much potential.

I wished I had the power to flash ahead 15-20 years to see where he ended up, because I was sure it would be somewhere wonderful. I won't forget him and I really hope life has treated him well.

7: Calypso Fever

We were into our second year fostering when Children's Aid approached us and asked if we would be willing to take on the responsibility of being the emergency shelter for the entire county. They also asked if we could officially act as a respite home for foster homes caring for special needs children, to give them a brief break from their work with kids requiring extra attention.

I'm not sure if this invitation was based on the fact that we had a lot of room and plenty of wide-open spaces or that we had been enjoying some success with troubled youth. Either way, it made a change in how we would be receiving some of the children.

We would continue to foster the usual kids who came our way, but we would now be getting calls at any time, day or night, to pick up or accept delivery of kids who had come into care but had not as yet been assessed. These would literally be emergency intakes and, depending on whether I was home or out running around, I could be picking kids up at the police station or hospital, or hooking up with a social worker somewhere in town.

They would also be delivered to our home in the middle of the night, and I got used to a routine in which these late-delivery kids would often be hungry and needed to be fed, cleaned up and comforted before I could put them to bed. They would not be off to school the next day and, together, we would wait for word from their social worker on the next step.

They were so desperate to know what was going to happen to them and I learned it was best to not share what little info I might have. So many things could affect how Children's Aid proceeded and it wasn't my call to hypothesize on any actions.

It was especially difficult to see how frightened so many of them were, not knowing what was ahead. Even if they had had a horrible life so far, it was the only one they knew and they still found comfort in the familiarity of it. Not knowing what was going to happen was sometimes more traumatizing to them than what they had already experienced.

Never was it more apparent to me that life just isn't fair.

One of the means of connecting us with Children's Aid was a pager. I had never used one before and it was embarrassing the first time it went off.

I happened to be pulling into a U-pick strawberry field with one of my teen girls, and my immediate response was to check the warning lights on the dash of my car. Not finding anything flashing and panic rising in my voice, I asked Kimberly if she knew what was wrong with the car.

She was laughing so hard she could hardly speak. Thank God she knew what a pager sounded like. I don't know how long I would have sat in that field before I figured it out on my own.

It was because of our new status as the emergency shelter that we first met Rob. He had just completed a sentence at a youth detention facility and, without ceremony, a worker picked him up at the bus station and drove him immediately out to our farm.

He was 17 and a half and there weren't a lot of resources being made available for him at this point. Not that there hadn't been over the years. He had been in care since he was two and had even been placed through the adoption program at one point. This had not worked out and he had been returned to care. So, within six months after arriving at our home, he would no longer be a ward of Children's Aid and would be set free as an independent adult.

I had enjoyed working with so many children in our first year, and this would be the first time I met a person I lost no love for. I say this with a guilt-free conscience.

Rob was very tall, well developed and thought very highly of himself. He seemed to think that all he had to do was smile through half closed eyes and he could have his way on any matter. He walked around with a half-sneer on his face and I immediately felt suspicious of his manner and decided I would have to keep my guard up at all times.

He had been in care before being sent away to detention and I asked for an opportunity to talk to his previous foster parents. They were very blunt in saying what a great guy he was, but don't let him go through your mail and get access to any account numbers. He had sold their phone info and managed to make some money for himself and somehow used their credit card numbers to secure stuff which he then sold. He was capable of stealing and pawning anything he could get his hands on.

But they stopped short of admitting the one thing that I will not forgive them for keeping from me.

As foster parents, we have a duty to protect ourselves and others when there is danger or a potential risk associated with a child. When I spoke to his previous foster mom, she failed to mention that he had been violent with her and she didn't report it because she didn't want him to get into any more trouble. This information was provided to me two years later at a foster parents' conference.

Not telling me at the time Rob came into our care was completely irresponsible of her and, because of that, she made it possible for this violent teen to gain admittance into our home. Apparently, he had grabbed her and shoved her into a wall when something had not been agreeable to him.

With this oversight she had put me and my family at risk in her effort to protect a dangerous teenager who was in size bigger than many men. She also hid relevant information from Children's Aid and made it impossible to properly prepare me for what might happen with his placement in our home.

I would soon find out.

The first signs of Rob being up to his old tricks were when he tried to find out what the password was for the computer. We allocated time for kids to go on the computer and the sites they could access were controlled.

We started to notice that when it was time for someone to go on, Rob would coincidentally slip outside for a cigarette. It took a couple of incidents before someone noticed him through the window, standing outside in the dark, trying to see through the dusty window panes when we input the password.

It was spooky at first, with his pale profile barely lit up by the interior lights. A dark jacket concealed his body and his disembodied head seemed to float across the panes as he desperately tried to make out what keys my husband hit to open access to the internet.

He tried this several times before he finally gave up.

An immediate issue we had with Rob was his penchant for profanity. We did not allow swearing in our house, but Rob explained to me, as only Rob could, that it was not possible for him not to swear. He spoke to me in his conniving manner as a teacher might explain the theory of relativity to a dullard. He felt he had been born with this abnormality and that it was so ingrained in his psyche that he couldn't carry on a conversation without dropping the 'f' bomb. He peppered every conversation with several of his favourite curses and he assured me I would just have to learn to live with it.

I had a different opinion and, after a lengthy discussion, I promised Rob I could show him he really did have control over his obscenities. I pretended this would be so exciting for us both.

I had always been fortunate in finding the Achilles' heel in kids when it came to adjusting behaviour. With Rob it was the time he spent on the phone.

He had developed quite a following of females who needed his constant attention, and I started off by telling him that, if the cursing continued, his telephone time would be restricted. The next time he swore, he would lose one day off the phone, the second time it would be two days and the third he would lose an entire week.

It probably *was* hard for him to stop, and I doubt he had ever been motivated as much before, so he lost the first day's access to the phone almost instantly. Within another day, he lost the second shift accessing the phone, and within a week he had the final punishment of losing his privileges for an entire week.

Miracle of all miracles, he stopped swearing.

For some reason, he did not share any sense of achievement in his success, and met my congratulations with an angry stare.

Despite my praises, the night he lost the full week of phone privileges was not without consequence to myself. I remember how his demeanour changed and the eyes that followed me around the room were dark and menacing.

The administration of his punishment took place just before bedtime and everything seemed normal as the kids wandered off.

When I eventually went up the stairs, I decided to make a quick call using the phone that sat just outside my bedroom door at the end of the hall. It was one of those old, grey plastic phones, flat with square numbers that had to be pressed to dial.

I noticed when I picked up the receiver that there was something slimy and wet all over my phone. It was viscous and smelt slightly of bleach.

It was on my fingers when the realization hit me—my phone was covered in semen.

I stifled a scream. This was an unfathomable level of depravity.

It didn't take a rocket scientist to figure out who had done it. Shrouded in darkness, he had stood outside my door and masturbated on my phone in retaliation for losing his telephone privileges.

How could anyone do something so disgusting? To express his anger in this manner made me feel we had a deeply disturbed person living with us. He must have been pretty pleased with himself.

Rob was a nasty young man, and I didn't really hold out much hope for his future. I couldn't even bring myself to talk to him about it.

I did let Children's Aid know what had happened and they pleaded with me that I try and hang on a few more weeks. They would try to find another placement, but with his resume, it wouldn't be easy.

On a positive note, we were very much enjoying Rob's new-found ability to control his language. I made a point of complimenting him about it every chance I got.

It was also about this time that I noticed how my cats were behaving around Rob. If he entered a room, they would quickly slink out, bellies low and flattened to the floor. He was doing something to my cats outside of my presence, and the way he looked at them was creepy, to say the least. I couldn't prove it but, in my mind, I begged that he do something in front of me. I may have used some profanity myself if I could catch him at it.

I was beginning to wonder if I was housing someone so damaged and disturbed that in later years he might blossom into a serial killer. My calls to Children's Aid to have him removed became more frequent.

When a situation arose in which I needed to confront any of the children with something that had happened, I would often invite the individual or individuals to go for a drive in our car. Once we were on the road, I would bring up the issue and, regardless as to how things went, I knew I had a captive audience. This took away their ability to dramatically storm out of a room, as most people don't jump out of a moving car.

In this way we could calmly talk about it, no matter how reluctant the kids were, as I asked for their side or invited their input. We could then work it out before I pulled back down into our driveway. I found it very effective.

Of course, after the first or second invitation, the kids knew the true meaning behind "Let's go for a drive."

I found out from one of the teens in our home that Rob had persuaded a twelve-year-old to hand over his weekly allowance so Rob could buy him cigarettes when he next went to town. With this information tucked quietly inside my mind, I invited both Rob and the younger kid to take a drive with me.

Once we were on the road, I let them know the real purpose of the drive. Again, I was always counting on no one being brave enough to tuck and roll out of the car.

Rob was definitely unhappy about the situation and, through the rear-view mirror, I could see him shooting the younger kid the evil eye for spilling the beans.

The consequence that I imposed was that the younger kid lost his allowance that week and Rob would not be going to town with the rest of us. And I made sure Rob knew I didn't get the information from the younger kid, although I don't know if that would have made a difference. I already understood Rob had a very twisted mind when it came to getting revenge.

Just when I didn't think Rob could sink any lower, he redefined low. While on a run into town with some of the kids to our mall, I ran into one of Rob's 'babes'. I knew her from the food bank and we got along pretty well so she felt comfortable telling me that in one of her lengthy chats with Rob, he told her it was his goal to get each and every kid in my home hooked on drugs before he left. This included Amanda, who already had more than her share of challenges in this world.

My calls to Children's Aid to have him removed were no longer pleading. I wanted him out by the end of the week or I would be dropping him off at their office. I had no doubt he had the connections to get his hands on whatever drugs he required. I have no idea where the money would come from and I can't say I was missing anything from our home. Rob was a motivated slime ball and would have found a way to make it happen.

Before the week was out, I was required to take Rob in for a meeting with his probation officer. I applied the same rules as I did when taking Cynthia to her appointments, making sure to deliver him to the right office.

For some reason on this day, I decided not to wait in the outer office for Rob to finish his session. I told him I would meet him at the car.

I sat there for over half an hour and then started to wonder where he might have got to. When I went to check on him, I found out he had already left, most likely by the back stairs.

I made no effort to drive around surrounding streets to find him. Concerns that I might have been derelict in my responsibilities couldn't have been farthest from my mind. In fact, as the realization settled in that he was gone, I actually started to feel joy slowly washing over me. Rob had run away and a weight was lifted off my shoulders.

It was still a forty-minute drive from home, but as each and every one of those minutes passed, my mood became lighter and lighter. By the time I arrived home, I practically exploded from the car.

Once inside, I made a beeline for the stereo and put on some of Harry Belafonte's music. As 'Jump in the Line' began to pulse out of the speakers, I turned it up and began to dance!

The rest of the kids quickly joined me, and I let them know what I was celebrating.

Rob had been nasty and cruel to kids and animals alike in my home. He had masturbated on my phone, hurt my pets, taken kids' allowances and threatened to turn my other children into addicts. There was something seriously wrong with him but he was no longer my concern. I was beyond caring if his heinous personality would ever find redemption.

It didn't matter to me that my opinion of him might forever be unsubstantiated. For me, his capacity for immorality was undeniable. I was done with him and, apparently, so was Children's Aid. I don't believe he was offered another placement, but I'm sure he would have received some support in his transition to independence. Last I heard, he was working as a roadie or hawker with a travelling fair that crossed the country. My sympathy is reserved for those who cross his path and I have no doubt he will forever be a menace to society.

Forgiveness is a release to the soul and I don't feel any ongoing resentment towards Rob. I'm just happy I'll never have to deal with him again.

8: Bad to the bone

Shane was an emergency placement to our home, scheduled to be with us a short two weeks before a court-ordered stay at our province's youth detention facility. He was 12 years old and had already accumulated a very thick file of recorded incidents and involvement with the local police and school administrators. He had been brought before a judge, who felt he had exhausted opportunities to correct his behaviour and that the detention facility was the avenue of last resort.

Shane was supposed to have passed this period of time with his family, but there had been an incident at his home that morning and his mother had demanded he be removed immediately. Instead, I was to hold him for those two weeks before he was to begin his sentence.

This would be a learning experience for me in that, no matter what assumptions we might make about a person, we never really know them. I based my opinion on information provided to me at the time.

Shane had already been expelled from school and also had some kind of restraining order preventing him from being near any school, playground or any-where children might gather. It was hard for me to get my head around a 12-year-old being barred from playgrounds, baseball fields, and similar spaces. Apparently, he was violent and deemed a high risk to other children. I wondered what I was letting into my home.

Shane was tall and good looking, with a dark mop of hair and deep brown eyes. He shuffled through my door wearing oversized jeans and a baggy T-shirt, head tilted down but eyes peering up through dishevelled hair. His manner was hostile but not rude when he was introduced to me.

The social worker offered a few more details about his situation and reiterated that this was just a temporary arrangement. She encouraged Shane to be on his best behaviour and I thought this was more than a little optimistic.

I immediately took Shane up to his room and tried to outline some of the house rules. He quickly became agitated and started to go on about how his uncle was going to come and get him and take him away from this place. I got the impression that the uncle was a force to be reckoned with.

Within minutes, he escalated to pounding his head with his fists and screaming that he wanted to go home. He was in a situation where he was no longer in control, and maybe hurting himself was a way of regaining some measure of it back.

I told him I thought my standing there was upset-ting him and that I was going to give him some privacy and some time to settle down. When he was ready, he could come downstairs and meet the other kids.

I was pretty sure we wouldn't see him for the rest of the evening, and I was truly shocked when he casually came down the stairs within ten minutes. He was more relaxed and maybe even a little resigned to his situation. I was amazed at how quickly he gained control and seemed to be moving forward with whatever was to come. Another example of just how resilient these kids can be when faced with adversity.

One of the last-minute instructions the social worker left me with was an amusing demand from Shane's mother that when I did his laundry, his jeans and T-shirts had to be washed separately. We're not talking about all the jeans in one batch and the T-shirts in another. She was insisting each individual article of clothing be washed independently of any other article.

She had apparently made sure all of Shane's clothes were top-of-the-line, name-brand garments. She did not want to risk the possibility that dye from one item might infiltrate another and of course ruin his valuable wardrobe.

That was a hard no from me, and I let the social worker know that it wasn't just because we were on a well and couldn't divert so much water to Shane's clothes. It was because I found the demand ludicrous and I wouldn't be a part of it.

There seemed to be a vibe coming from the social

worker that we needed to appease Shane's mother. This was the beginning of a challenging relationship.

Shane seemed to be settling in and immediately developed a friendship with my daughter. What I really mean is, he did his best to try and intimidate her and, like water rolls off a duck's back, she ignored him.

He was still warning us of the impending arrival of his uncle, but at no time did he physically threaten anyone.

My daughter was 16 at the time and usually met Shane's attempts to unnerve with laughter. She was very assertive in her own right and nothing he did or said bothered her. She often rebuffed his commentary with quick wit and snappy comebacks, often leaving him looking quite silly. I sometimes would overhear them playing Nintendo and there was a lot of ass kicking being tossed around, but all in good nature.

It was also my relief that Shane wasn't bothering the other kids in our home. I found it odd that Shane had been barred from schoolyards and playgrounds, but here he didn't seem interested in engaging any of the kids, with the exception of typical youth trash talking.

Shane's mother was allowed to call our home and he wasn't long with us before she asked to speak to me. She had placed an order with Sears for some clothing Shane needed and now that he was no longer in her custody, someone else had to pick them up and pay for them. She went on at length about how she would no longer be receiving her family allowance for him so it would be up to me to cover the cost of whatever she had ordered.

I found out much later that she 'forgot' to inform Family Allowance administrators that she was short one kid, and continued to collect money in Shane's name for the next two years.

I am a control freak and, although Children's Aid did provide a clothing allowance for kids in care, it was up to my discretion how that money would be spent. His mother was not happy when I told her I wasn't interested in paying for the purchases she thought were essential.

I had already seen the clothes Shane wore and they looked great, but were very expensive. When the allowance was approximately $300 for four months, I wasn't about to spend $200 on a pair of jeans.

I told Shane's mother I would get my husband to pick up the Sears package and if they were items, he needed, I would pay for them. I was alienating her but it didn't matter much. Shane would only be with me another week and she could see how far her demands would get at the detention facility.

My husband went into town the next day and, when he checked out the package at Sears, it was a large bundle of younger kids' clothing, including some items for a little girl. He left the parcel where it was and I called Shane's mom to let her know that Sears had offered a bundle of the wrong items. She went off on a tangent about the incompetence of sales clerks in general and even hinted that my husband wasn't all the swift and should have asked for the other package waiting for pick-up.

The next day, my husband went back to town and tried once again to pick up Shane's clothing. The staff at Sears insisted there was no other package and the one with the various sizes was the only one they had.

When I called Shane's mother with the news, I started to get the impression that rage was her default setting. She didn't hold back this time, telling me what she thought of the staff at Sears. Then she told me my husband was an idiot and somebody had better get in there and pay for those clothes.

It surprised me just how quickly she had attempted to scam us into paying for an order of clothing for her younger three children. I wasn't about to be bullied into cooperating with her scheme and this really made her angry. But again, Shane was about to leave us, so there wasn't any use in making an issue of it.

Unfortunately, things were about to get complicated.

After Shane's first week, his social worker suggested I try sending him to our local school just to give him something to occupy himself. He was still scheduled to head off within the next week or two, but the whole situation seemed to be somewhat fluid.

The teacher assigned to Shane's class was a petite spitfire of a women who could have easily passed for a ten-year-old. To underestimate her would be a mistake, as she was very much in control of her students and, although Shane may have been disruptive, there was nothing she couldn't deal with.

The progress that had been made at our home was complemented by initial good reports coming from the school. With his new school firmly prepared to accept Shane despite his history, Children's Aid made an appeal to the courts, it was decided he would be staying with us for the foreseeable future.

I knew Shane was going to be a handful but, at the same time, I thought there was a lot of promise in him. Relations with his mother, however, would be another story.

A few weeks later we were still getting to know each other and I was gradually learning more about Shane's family. My daughter was getting along well with him and he confided to her that he used to play a game with his uncle called 'Hitler'. They would catch flies, pull off their wings and burn them with cigarette butts. The uncle had been playing this game with him ever since he was quite young and Shane very much enjoyed it.

What an iconic example of how to screw up a kid's psyche. Twisted and sick, this had to have contributed something to Shane's development and it provided a window into his family life.

Shane was doing well at school so far, and for him to not use his fists was a real accomplishment. I give this credit to his teacher and the principal at that time, who were both no-nonsense types, quick to nip anything in the bud before it had time to develop.

Despite their attention, there were still going to be incidents, and the first one literally caused me to stop breathing when I heard.

I got a phone call from the principal telling me one of the kids in gym class had taken Shane's expensive shoes and flushed them in the toilet. They didn't go down, of course, but they had definitely had a bath and Shane had been kept from reacting with the assurance that it would be dealt with. I don't know why the kid did this, but he must have had a death wish.

The principal had already contacted the kid's parents and Shane's shoes were going to be replaced immediately. They weren't cheap by any means, because his mother had always insisted, he have the best.

The school handled this issue quickly and efficiently and I was hoping Shane learned something about conflict resolution. I might have been overly optimistic. We were still dealing with a 12-year-old who had been conditioned to meet adversity in the most threatening physical means possible.

I spoke with Children's Aid about Shane's frequent referencing of his uncle and how we all had better watch out. Shane very much looked up to him and a lot of his violent behaviour was somehow designed to please his uncle.

His social worker had met the uncle and found him pleasant and agreeable. The uncle had had run-ins with local law enforcement and had never been uncooperative with them. From all reports, he was pretty complacent but could be a nuisance when drunk.

I couldn't fathom how Shane had an image of his uncle being a deadly force to reckon with, but it had to do with family dynamics and how the uncle conducted himself around his nephew.

Although the sneaker situation had been dealt with, there were still other events happening in the classroom with Shane's behaviour and he eventually received his first suspension of one day.

Much to his disappointment, I had a policy that if a kid was suspended from school, the moment they would normally walk out my door to catch the school bus was the moment they started working. There was no sleeping in or laying around the house playing video games.

There was wood to stack, gardens to dig, animals to feed, etc. He would get a break and lunch time that equalled school time allotments, but work didn't stop until when he would have normally got off the school bus coming home. There was no free ride and I hoped it might give him something to consider when acting up at school. This made the prospect of a day at home much worse that the privilege of staying in class.

Unfortunately, this strategy didn't have quite enough of an impact on Shane.

Occasionally, there were slight conflicts between my personal policies and those of Children's Aid. An issue that had always bothered me was their approach towards kids smoking.

Shane smoked when he had cigarettes and, although I didn't allow smoking inside my home, I was not to interfere with it when they went outside. It was Children's Aids theory that these kids usually had a lot of turmoil in their lives and dealing with a smoking addiction was not high on the priority list.

With that, I simply asked that cigarette butts be thrown in the wood stove and not create litter around the outside of the house. I was otherwise not to interfere with their habit unless the kid was younger than 12.

One day it was raining when Shane stepped out on the porch to smoke a cigarette. I didn't watch the kids when they did this so I didn't notice when he wandered away down towards the poultry barn.

Within minutes, though, Shane came running up the hill screaming, "The turkey's on fire! The turkey's on fire!"

There was so much urgency in his voice, we immediately knew this wasn't a prank. My husband was quick getting his boots on and made it to the barn in lightning speed.

Apparently, Shane had decided to get out of the rain and have his smoke in the turkey enclosure. While he was standing with his cigarette dangling down past his hip, a turkey had walked up to him and grabbed the lit cigarette, swallowing it before Shane could react. It instantly started gobbling loudly in distress, with smoke rippling out its nostrils and beak.

It was a sight out of a Merrie Melodies cartoon.

Shane was visibly upset and my husband quickly grabbed some water and poured it down the turkey's gullet, putting out the embers smouldering in its crop (this is a little pouch down a turkey's neck that contains gravel and is used to help grind up seeds). The cigarette had ignited some of the remnants in the crop and was easily put out when the water was flushed down its throat.

As hysterical as the scene might have appeared, I was very upset that Shane had chosen to have his cigarette in a wooden barn full of hay. If a fire had started, it would have been seconds before the entire structure would have been engaged and no guarantees that Shane could have made it out in time. I reprimanded him at length about the danger and hoped the message got through.

Despite the seriousness of the incident, it has been many years and I still can't forget the image of that turkey with smoke billowing out of its nostrils.

There was never a dull moment when it came to Shane. A couple of months into the school year, I received a call late in the afternoon from the mother of a family further down the road from where we lived. She told me Shane had walked up to her eight-year-old girl in the school playground and threat-ened to beat her up. The playground was divided into two sections with grades 1-4 on one side and 5-7 on the other.

I told her I would talk to Shane and get to the bottom of what was going on. This kind of stunt fit Shane like a glove and I had no doubt he was guilty

—shame on me.

I decided I needed to talk to him and get his side of the story before I could measure out a consequence. Shane had often been blamed for this kind of activity, but I had to explore the possibility that he might be innocent.

I called him into the kitchen, where I was in the middle of making supper. I sat him down and related the phone call I had received and asked him if it was true. It was important to me that I not use an accusatory tone and that we talked calmly without raising any voices.

Shane was brief with his response. He denied having anything to do with the little girl let alone approaching her in the school yard. He was calm and collected and it left me feeling I needed to go further.

So now I was presented with a situation. Despite Shane's reputation for intimidation and aggressive behaviour, there was no way I could punish a kid for something they didn't do. It was also important that Shane and I discuss the issue without escalating the situation with loud voices.

Shane cooperated 100%, keeping his own voice even and his depiction of events clear and concise.

I turned off all the burners on the stove and got back on the phone. I called the mother down the road and asked if I could have the names and numbers of at least three of her daughter's friends who would have been with her when this happened. I then called Shane back into the room and asked for names of a couple of the kids he was hanging out with that day.

With my list in hand, I started to make phone calls. Each number I called, I explained the situation and asked for permission to speak to their child.

Not everyone was in agreement with my direct contact, but they did bring their child to the phone and relayed my questions. This delayed our supper by well over an hour and I was left alone to bring the truth to light. Shane deserved no less and after his already muddied history, I somehow felt it was even more important that I not contribute to the anger he seemed to have accumulated over the years.

I managed to get through to everyone I wanted to talk to and both the little girl's friends and Shane's buddies gave the exact same account. Shane had not approached the little girl and had certainly not spoken to her that day. It was a complete fabrication on her part and I was now left with informing her mother.

Before I called her, I took a moment to try to figure out why this whole thing had happened in the first place. Shane had seen her on the bus every day but had not had much contact with her that he could recall. I could imagine Shane being his usual self, interacting with other kids and perhaps this might have come across threatening to her?

I was glad the little girl's mother was accepting of my conclusion and we talked about how the girl might be a little afraid of Shane and might somehow be looking for a safeguard from her parents.

I called Shane back into the kitchen and let him

know the results of whole mess and that he was to give this little girl a wide birth. He didn't understand why she was scared, but was glad things worked out the way they did. I don't regret for one moment taking the time to find the truth.

Shane had been with us three months now and I was starting to notice a pattern in his behaviour. Often, after he had a phone call from his mother, he would walk away and punch a door or start yelling at someone. There was a lot of anger and it stemmed from his conversations with her.

I had no idea what they talked about but she sure knew how to push his buttons. We still didn't have a complete picture of Shane, but his mother seemed to contribute to some of his more challenging behaviour. I had to wonder how many of those other incidents in his file had followed an exchange with her.

Christmas was coming and Shane's social worker approached me about Shane staying with us over the holidays. His mother was going off with her boyfriend for a few days. The social worker also asked if we would be willing to take in his younger sister for Christmas and Boxing Day. His mother's other two children were spending the holidays with their biological fathers and she was left with one child who had nowhere to go. Her boyfriend was not the family man type and apparently had no interest in her children.

I agreed to this, as long as they arranged for the transportation to bring Shane's sister out on Christmas Day. I had mixed feelings about this whole situation, but Shane was looking forward to having his sister with him, even though he would not be getting together with his mother and other siblings.

It was just after one pm on the 24th when I got a cheerful call from Shane's mother. She was full of Christmas spirit as she asked me when I was coming in to pick up Shane's sister. She was anxious to get on the road for her get-away with her boyfriend.

I told her this wasn't the arrangement I had agreed to. She was a day early.

She criticized the social workers for their incompetence in not letting me know I actually had Shane's younger sister for a more extended period of time, starting immediately. She thought that, because it was 1 pm, everyone would have left the office and I wouldn't be able to get hold of social services.

"This has already been set up and they just forgot to tell you!" she bubbled over the phone. She then proceeded to tell me the workers were all gone for the holidays now and asked again when I was coming in, as she had to take off for her Christmas.

I don't think she had thought this one through very well. Children's Aid has to have someone on call day or night, any time of year, and I immediately got a hold of the worker on duty. It took a little digging, as she wasn't Shane's social worker, but she did confirm that we were not supposed to get his sister till the next day.

How could a mother try to dump their own child on Christmas Eve? This most magical of holidays made for families to celebrate and enjoy, yet she couldn't push her kids out the door fast enough.

Children's Aid was happy to nip this in the bud, and she was made to hang on till the next day. We were happy to receive our guest as previously arranged. Shane and his sister would spend the next couple of days exploring around the farm and having a good time together.

I'm glad we were available to have his sibling with us, but I resented Shane's mother trying to take advantage of us.

The new year had all the kids back in school, and Shane had not lost his ability draw negative attention. He was soon receiving the occasional suspension, sometimes for one day, sometimes for two. Eventually, I started to run out of work to have him do around the farm.

I still wasn't going to have him sitting around, so I came up with the idea that he could start baking bread. I taught him how to read a recipe, and I realized the physical aspect of kneading was a great way for him to burn up excess energy.

He enjoyed the process of pounding his fists into the dough and he was very proud of the results. It turned out Shane was a natural when it came to baking, and we were more than happy to have fresh, homemade bread for supper.

He was also very shy when it came to compliments and it made him uncomfortable to hear what a good job, he did at anything.

It had been a while since Shane's last suspension, and I had been lulled into a false sense of peace and tranquility. Then the phone rang and I was totally taken off guard. I couldn't make sense of what I was hearing at the other end of the line. There was sputtering, stuttering and a lot of garbled static. It almost sounded like someone was being strangled.

It turned out to be the principal from Shane's school, and she was more than a little agitated. It was a minute or two before I could make out any actual words. She was still struggling to convey details, but I clearly got the message that Shane was suspended for a week.

Usually, the suspension of a child for an entire week required approval from the school board, but she wasn't looking for a second opinion. She was not a woman to be trifled with at this point.

I slowly started to get a clearer picture of what had happened. Shane's elementary school had been chosen to host a teachers' conference and the principal was proud to show off her school. Educators from the entire county had descended on the school to share and inspire each other.

The principal was out front welcoming arrivals when Shane did one of the dumbest things he had done to date. Another student made the poor decision to bring a water gun to school. Not a little squirt pistol but one of the super soaker varieties and it was fully loaded when a couple of Shane's friends dared him to hit the principal.

She saw it coming and warned him from a distance, but that short circuit in Shane's decision-making failed him once again. He nailed her full on and in front of the visiting participants of the conference. The humiliation was too much to bear and she completely lost her composure.

I had had dealings with her before and she had always been stoic and firm. He reduced her to a raving lunatic in a manner of seconds.

So, Shane was at home again, stacking wood and baking bread. He had become resigned to his fate and, for some strange reason, never argued about his consequences. He may have whined and complained from time to time, but he still did as he was asked.

Coinciding with the week of Shane's suspension, I had a luncheon for staff from the food bank and Shane helped set out the food, including some of his wonderful bread. Everyone was very impressed with how helpful he was and how lucky I was to have him with me. If only they knew.

It was a paradox that he had been sent home after 'ruining' the principals' conference (slightly exaggerated) and now was helping me host my own gathering. I let him know I appreciated the good job he was doing, even if this was still a punishment. He blushed at the praise from our visitors and tried to hide in the kitchen, but I do think he liked being noticed for something good. He just wasn't used to it.

Two days later, the principal called and apologized for overreacting. Shane's suspension was reduced to time served, which had been only two days at that point. He was welcome to return the next day and, although the incident was far from forgotten, everyone was going to move forward.

The principal then shared something about Shane's reaction to suspensions. On a previous infraction, the principal had called him into the office and she told him he was being sent home, he had broken down and cried. He went on at length about how hard I made him work and he was just a slave on the farm.

I was indifferent to the revelation. If things were all that horrible, he should make more of an effort to behave. I let the principal know my policies would not be changing, but to let me know if she noticed a change or worsening in Shane's behaviour. I wasn't trying to destroy his spirit, but he had just turned 13 and, previous to coming to our home, had led a life devoid of any structure or discipline. He had been plucked from the edge of calling a youth detention facility his home, so I wasn't feeling guilty about my rules.

As it turned out, the water spraying suspension was the last one Shane experienced that school year. I don't know if it was due to an improvement in behaviour or if the school decided to go a little easier on him. Whatever the reason, I think we were both pleased that things finally seemed to settle down.

Spring was soon upon us and, with the blossoming of flowers, so too did Shane's interest peak in a local girl not far from our farm. I knew he was interested in spending some time with her, so I suggested they take their bikes and go to a nearby waterfall. Shane had recently baked some bread, not because of a suspension but because he liked to do it.

I suggested he could make some sandwiches and show her what his skill could produce and he was immediately resistant. There's no way he wanted her to know he had made the loaf. It was disappointing that he saw this as effeminate, and I wasn't successful persuading him otherwise but he did take the sandwiches with him.

My daughter knew the girl Shane was interested in seeing because she happened to be the sister of my daughter's boyfriend. Despite the idyllic scenery and clumsy banter, things had deteriorated after what had started out to be a perfectly lovely afternoon.

My daughter got a firsthand account of how Shane had suddenly started calling the girl some absolutely terrible names. She wasn't sure what had sent him off, but he also was quite casual in using the profanity, as if it meant nothing at all.

She had left him on the bank of the stream and he didn't seem to think he had done anything wrong. He was the one who had invited her out and it was disconcerting how he had sabotaged their little date.

When he got back home, I took him aside and asked him how everything went. He didn't detail the name-calling but told me she got pissed off with him and left. I let him know she had called and that I had heard a different version. He didn't deny cursing at her but he thought it was just fooling around and she had taken unjustified offence.

He didn't seem to know how to express himself in this awkward situation, and I let him know these

145

were not terms any girl or woman wants to hear.

He still seemed confused. What was the big deal?

I tried to get through to him that this wasn't just my personal opinion. I don't think this was a learning opportunity for him, as he just shrugged his shoulders and walked away.

He really liked this girl but he had expressed his discomfort in such an inappropriate way, I wasn't sure she would ever spend time with him again.

Shane was scheduled for a visit with his family on a weekend in May, involving an overnight and an opportunity to see his grandmother. She was a big part of his life and they both meant a lot to each other.

When Shane returned that Sunday afternoon, he paused as he came through the front door and reached into his backpack. He hesitated before he gently pulled a gun out of his bag and handed it over to me.

It was shiny, black and heavy, and I don't think I've ever been so horrified. It looked quite real and I didn't know enough about guns to recognize what type it was. All I knew was that it was a hand gun and not a toy for a 13-year-old. His family felt otherwise.

"My grandmother gave this to me because she thought I might want to kill something while I'm here." his eyes were downcast and I could tell he wasn't comfortable with this confession.

There were times I worried about Shane's future and other times I was so very proud of him. This was one of those moments when I felt we were really get-

ting somewhere and seeing improvements in responsible behaviour. I know his grandmother was
suggesting Shane try hunting the wildlife around the
farm, but he knew we weren't about using living
creatures for target practice.

It turned out to be only a BB gun, but was still
capable of hurting animals or people, and I was so
happy Shane had enough sense to realize this was
not going to be acceptable. He went on to say he
knew it was something I didn't approve of and
seemed relieved to be giving the gun over to me.

I don't think he had asked for anything like this
and was quite happy to be rid of it. I was outraged
that the grandmother would give him a gun to bring
into my home. The picture into his home life was
getting clearer. I had zero empathy for these people
and their lifestyle and I knew a lot more about them
than what Children's Aid had provided, and I did not
have a positive opinion of them.

Despite the occasional trouble Shane could get
into at school, there was so much promise in other
behaviour he displayed at home. Shane had participated in the egg incubation project and from it, he had
hatched out a male Muscovy duck that he became
very attached to. He named it Butthead. Shane was
also the source for me naming my duck Corn olio.

Butthead grew up that spring and Shane could often be seen wandering around outside with his duck
in tow. Sometimes he would just sit on a hill with his
arm around the duck and they both seemed so much
at peace. Butthead had such a pleasant personality

and even went so far as to play tag with my husband.

My husband would be coming up from feeding the poultry and Butthead would sneak up behind him and nip him on the leg. My husband would then chase him back down the hill and this back and forth could go on for several minutes.

We decided Butthead would be a permanent resident of the farm and never end up on the dinner table.

It was Easter when I decided to visit my family in the Valley for a day. Shane was the only child with us as others in our home had taken the opportunity to spend Easter with their relatives.

My family was very supportive of what we were doing and, when we arrived, the men folk were getting ready to head out and do some fishing. It was unexpected when they invited Shane to come along and try his luck and I hesitated, wondering what risk there might be for something to go wrong. He was my responsibility and if anything went wrong, I would be accountable.

Shane seemed keen on the idea of catching a fish and I decided to let him go and, I hoped have a good time. The group included my father, brother and two step brothers, all very experienced fishermen.

I spent the afternoon helping my step mother and step sister prepare Easter dinner, with the usual bustling, comforting activities that bond us in our exertions. Several hours passed and eventually the men returned, but the mood was sombre and perhaps even a little hostile.

I immediately started beating myself up for even thinking it had been a good idea to send Shane out with them. I had put everyone in jeopardy by letting him go and now something had happened to ruin the day for us all.

My brother spoke up first, loudly declaring how ungrateful Shane was as a guest on their little fishing trip. Then my father piped up to tell me they would never invite him along again because of how he had made them all look like fools.

I looked at Shane and his head was down, but I noticed the corners of his mouth were quivering. He didn't look at all apologetic and his face suddenly erupted in a big grin.

My brother described how Shane was the only one who caught any fish that day, much to the humiliation of all the experienced anglers. Shane had caught three nice trout, which my step brother finally hoisted up high for us all to admire.

They all had a good time teasing Shane about his prowess, and it was obvious that Shane had had an amazing time. They really got me good by pretending he had pulled off a stunt, and it was a while before relief finally settled in. I very much appreciated my family welcoming Shane into their fold and seeing him swaggering around with such a wide smile really filled my heart.

The school year ended and, on the last day, all the kids came home and decided to make a ceremony of burning up all their school supplies. Shane led the charge in grabbing handfuls of paper and scribblers to toss into the wood stove and I knew how much had been spent to provide the materials. Children's Aid provided a school supply allowance that was quite healthy and the kids knew they would be getting all new stuff come September.

I saw the destruction of last year's goods a pure waste and jumped in with an offer I hoped would encourage them to be more frugal. For every item they hung onto and recycled for the new school year, I would compensate them with a trip to a go-kart speedway not too far from us. The more they saved, the more time they would get to spend racing each other around the race track.

It worked, and I was happy to see the kids bagging up their supplies and tucking them away for the end of summer.

Within a few months, summer was upon us and I continued to look for activities to occupy my brood. Within a half hour drive existed a drive-in movie theatre which played on weekends and always offered two recently-released films. They charged by the car so it was no problem for me to load up five kids and head out for an enjoyable, inexpensive evening.

It was on one of these outings that something unusual happened with Shane.

After I settled the car into position to see the huge screen, several of the teens went over to the canteen to check out the snacks. There was an arcade inside the building and a lot of local youth had congregated there, as young people do.

My group was interacting with them, and I can't say how well behaved they were, but one of the locals decided he wanted to start a fight with Shane. He swung his first punch but Shane tipped his head to one side and the blow glanced off his cheek.

This sent Shane into a fit of laughter and the other teen tried again with another swing that landed nowhere. Shane ridiculed the youth to the point where he simply backed up and was swallowed up by the crowd. No one took his place and the whole thing dissolved in seconds.

Everyone was so excited to tell me what had happened when they got back to the car. Shane had responded to someone else's aggression by laughing, and he wasn't at all disturbed by the incident. If this had happened a year ago, I don't think things would have gone well for the kid who had targeted Shane.

I can't say who started it—it may very well have been Shane getting mouthy—but I believe he was in control and chose not to respond with violence. A lot had changed over the last year.

Shane had started opening up to me, and sometimes we had quiet little chats. It was during one of these talks that he confessed he had lost his virginity to an older girl he knew the year before he came into foster care. He would have 11 at the time and she also was a minor, possibly 14 years herself.

I then made the mistake of letting this info slip out when I was having a casual exchange with his mother. She was cautioning me that Shane was taking more of an interest in girls and that I should keep a close watch, because she didn't want him losing his virginity.

"Yeah, well, that boats already sailed. You're two years late too worry about it now." I think I was a little resentful that she saw fit to give me parental advice.

The worst thing was that I had violated Shane's confidence. His mother was upset and wanted details, but I told her she would have to talk to Shane. It was bad enough that I had let the cat out of the bag.

As soon as I could get Shane alone, I apologized and told him I had messed up big time. He did not get angry with me and acted like it wasn't a situation he was happy about but that he would deal with. I was so sorry to have blindsided him with this, but his manner was forgiving and I didn't hear any more about it.

During the entire time that we were fostering at the farm, we found a lot of friends and family making the trek out to visit, have a meal and sometimes stay over. All of these guests took an interest in the children, and the kids responded by making people feel welcome and comfortable. It wasn't that I and my family had visitors; it was that the entire home had visitors and kids were an integral part of the experience.

If we did anything, we did it all together, whether it be going out for a walk, playing a game, or working on a craft or hobby. In this way, any and all of the children with us were included and shared hosting responsibilities.

It wasn't unusual to see kids taking guests on a tour to show off our garden or the poultry barns. I can remember Shane introducing people to the apple orchard when the trees were heavy with bright red fruit. He would reach up, twisting off a huge apple and crunching into its juicy flesh. With a mouth still occupied with chewing, he let them know anyone could come out anytime and just help themselves. I think it gave them a sense of satisfaction to be sharing what they knew about living on a farm.

When it was time for guests to leave, my husband and I always went out on the porch to say our good-byes and see them off till they were out of sight at the top of the hill. I was surprised to notice that Shane would come out and stand beside us, waving until they were gone. No words, just the waving of an arm and then he would silently turn and go back to whatever he was doing.

Shane never missed a 'wave-off' and I often wondered what he felt that motivated him to be a part of the farewell. None of the other kids did it but Shane would just slide out to join us and interrupt whatever he was up to. I told myself it was because he felt very much a part of the farm and took some ownership in the tranquility and harmony, we all felt there, and I was so happy to share that with him.

Gradually Shane was getting to spend more and more time with his family. His mother continued to aggravate him and he would often return to us angry and worked up. It would take him a couple of hours to settle down and I have no idea what was happen-

153

ing during the time he spent with her.

Children's Aid was working to have him returned permanently and everyone believed he had matured and was of a better disposition than when he first entered care a year ago.

We were always looking for activities that would help build confidence and provide a physical outlet for any stress or frustrations. Shane was doing well in school sports and seemed a natural for just about anything he turned his attention to, but didn't seem interested in joining any organized teams.

Children's Aid was always supportive of activities I enrolled the kids in and, after a lot of nudging, Shane expressed an interest in learning how to play the drums. I managed to find an instructor in town and Children's Aid willingly purchased a second-hand set of drums for a reasonable price of $400.

Shane started his lessons and the kids went to work clearing out the garage to create their own space and a home for the drums. There was no way the drums were getting into the house!

Once cleaned up, the old building was perfect as a hangout. We found a second-hand couch to install and the kids used their own money to purchase a cooler and several cases of soft drinks.

I had no concerns about them spending time out there and I did not closely supervise them, even when they had friends over. I was trusting in the kids being responsible and had explained that the moment something inappropriate happened, it would be all over.

It was at this time that I received a call from the head of Children's Aid and the care coordinator to say that something serious had happened and I had some explaining to do. They arrived in a sombre mood and definitely made it clear this was not a social call.

Everything was being spearheaded by the CEO. She started off by reminding me of my responsibilities as a foster parent. I didn't think I needed a refresher course, especially since a lot of kids were coming through my door, they kept asking me to become a parent counsellor and I had also been invited to train new foster parents in their orientation classes. If they had concerns about what I was doing, they might have mentioned it before now.

This wasn't about my general behaviour in looking after foster children: there was a specific incident they needed to discuss with me. Apparently, Shane had accessed marijuana and was known to have become high while he was in town. I was reprimanded for not keeping a closer eye on him and for not taking my care and control responsibilities more seriously. This was a major infraction and was going to affect my reputation and standing within the Children's Aid Society.

I agreed that this was devastating not only to our home and what we represented, but also to Children's Aid as the primary guardians of children in their care.

They then proceeded to ask me how it was that I had allowed this to happen and why I hadn't noticed the change in his behaviour when he was high. I needed more information, because I couldn't for the life of me understand what had taken place.

As soon as the supervisor identified the weekend in question, something tickled my brain. I had to ask again when exactly this had taken place. When she confirmed the date, a wave of relief washed over me. I was so anxious to correct this misunderstanding and protect my reputation as a foster parent.

"Shane wasn't with me that weekend—he was with his mother."

It was like watching someone at a high-stakes poker game. The CEO's face remained frozen but her eyes were flickering ever so slightly. I waited for the acknowledgement that this was a relief to us all and we could relax and take a deep breath.

She paused only briefly. It was as if she had re-hearsed her rebuke and needed to stay on script. I had caught her off guard, there was a slight stammer now in the words intended to chastise.

I couldn't believe she was continuing the condemnation of my behaviour, and I interrupted, "If he wasn't in my care, he wasn't in yours, either."

I was trying to push back a little and give them a chance to realize they had made a big mistake. I had nothing to feel guilty about and I was pretty sure they were just as innocent. But why were they being so steadfast in passing judgment?

"Incidentally, who reported Shane getting drugs in the first place?" I asked out of curiosity.

It was his mother who had informed Children's

Aid that I had corrupted him. So, Shane accessed drugs while in her care and she reported me as the culprit. What an unbelievably outrageous stunt to pull off. His mother was not up to the task of keeping Shane in line and she must have resented how well things had gone while in our care. Why not try to tarnish what we had accomplished with him?

But why was Children's Aid so eager to accept responsibility on my behalf? This entire thing could have easily been avoided if they had just checked the calendar.

What disappointed me the most about this circus was that I did not receive an apology. Instead, I was again reminded about the risks of not supervising kids closely and not a whisper about the job I was doing with the spectrum of behaviourally challenged children consigned to my care. The CEO continued to repress any acknowledgement of an error as she stood up and prepared to leave.

I asked if anything was going to be done about the false report Shane's mother had called in, but I didn't get the impression they wanted it to go any further. I felt I was being swept under the rug.

Shane was with us for another few weeks, and then full custody was returned to his mother. With her ability to wind him up, I feared he might slip back to his old behaviours. I trusted Shane had proven he was capable of controlling his behaviour in avoiding physical conflicts. I think he was always going to be the guy who doesn't back down from a dare and is sometimes impulsive.

I was pleasantly surprised to not hear any negative reports over the next few years and that things did go easier for him in the future.

Two months after Shane left us, a mother and her teenage boy showed up at our farm and explained to me they were there to pick up the drums. I didn't know who they were but they were polite but quite disappointed when I explained to them the drums didn't belong to me and I couldn't let them go for any price.

Apparently, Shane had sold the drums to this family and I had to tell them the drums actually belonged to Children's Aid and weren't available. This seemed like more a stunt his mother would pull off, so, to avoid any other disappointed buyers, I took the drums into Children's Aid to do with as they wished. There might be another kid interested in learning or they might just hand them over to Shane, but it would be their decision, not mine.

So, with finality, both Shane and his drums were gone from us and we missed the adventure he had brought into our lives. I learned that every kid needs a chance to prove themselves and Shane definitely proved he was so much more than a file folder full of reports.

9: It takes a village

I wake up from a dream that stays with me and doesn't immediately dissolve as I shake loose the cobwebs from a deep sleep.

In my dream, I'm in the kitchen getting the kids ready for school, packing lunches and making sure bags are loaded. Everything seems normal as they step off the porch and form a small stream meandering up the driveway towards the top of the hill. The pasture wheat is tall and mature as it ripples in the breeze, forming a soft, feathery gauntlet on both sides of the path.

As my eyes study the undulating patterns dancing across the wheat fields, I suddenly notice a break in the soft, golden waves. Something is moving out in the grass but I can't quite make it out.

Then I notice another abnormality on the opposite side of the meadow. The moving objects form a V as they move in the direction of the children, who are unaware they are being stalked. I suddenly realize the ghostly shapes are African lions and I watch motionless as they close in on their prey.

I remember being quite passive and thinking that it didn't really matter so much if a couple of the kids

159

were taken down. Children's Aid would simply send out some more to replace them. There would always be more children.

I open my eyes, shocked at my own indifference even if it was just in a dream. I had been so complacent and accepting of something horrific and terrifying. And as the dream prophesied, the children did keep coming.

One girl came to us under very sad circumstances. She had run away from home and was living with an uncle in a shack in the woods. Sandra had been exchanging sex for money with the uncle, and the upsetting part was that she had no problem with the arrangement. If the uncle had a visitor, she was conditioned to offer services to them as well. She had reluctantly been removed from the situation and landed at our home while Children's Aid sorted out more permanent arrangements and therapy.

Sandra was cheerful, with a vulgar sense of humour that needed to be cautioned from time to time. She wasn't with us long enough to be enrolled in school, so she spent her days home with me.

I could see she wasn't all that familiar with women or general household practices. It all seemed like a lot of unnecessary work to her, and managing a house held no appeal.

One of the other kids told me that Sandra had asked if she could find her a pimp. She wanted to prostitute herself but wasn't familiar with our area and was eager to make some money.

Sandra was 16 and this was the map she had laid

out for herself. Money would give her some independence and I had a feeling she had plans to run away from any home she might be placed in. Her life had been tainted from such an early age and there wasn't much for her to look forward to. She thought the other kids in our home were losers for attending school and living a normal life. I was so sad for her: without some serious intervention, her life held little promise.

Sandra did like to poke fun. One of my pet peeves was having to peel the little stickers off fruit before I ate it. I walked into the living room one afternoon to find a delicious apple plastered with stickers. They had removed every sticker she could find from the other fruit in the bowl, and raided the fridge, to concentrate them on one single apple. I pretended to flip out about the stickers violating my precious apple and the kids enjoyed their trick.

Sandra's next trick wasn't so amusing.

Sandra had already left to be placed with a family in what we hoped might be a more lasting situation. She may have been gone, but her presence was still being felt.

My fruit bowl was the victim again, and I couldn't understand why all the kids snickered and giggled when I picked up a plum and ate it. My hand became a Geiger counter, and every time I waved it near the fruit bowl, snickers erupted into laughter.

With some prodding, I managed to coax one of the kids into spilling the beans. Sandra had apparently taken each piece of fruit and wiped her rear end with it. She had literally pulled down her jeans and ran the fruit between the cheeks of her arse in full view of everyone there (no adults, obviously). I was more than a little disappointed that no one thought enough of me to tell me before I ate the plum.

I'm not a wasteful person, so I packaged up the contents of the bowl and mailed it to her at her new residence. I included a brief note: 'Glad you enjoyed our fruit!'

I also called her new foster mom and let her know what was happening. I didn't want to risk the new family consuming what I had sent, which would have had Sandra in hysterics, I'm sure. I know this was immature on my part, but I was desperate to retaliate in some way. Weak as it was, it gave me a tiny bit of satisfaction.

Then there was a young boy delivered to us in near-feral condition. Ryan was in desperate need of a bath and some clean clothes and, once I had him tidied up, I asked him if he would like a roast beef sandwich. He had no idea what roast beef or a sandwich was.

I found this a little hard to believe and kept asking him about other types of sandwiches. 'Nope' was his response to my queries and it seemed he was unfamiliar with a lot of things most of us take for granted. He also had no idea how to use utensils or even sit comfortably at a table.

It was Christmas and I had the tree set up in the dining room. The room assigned to Ryan was directly over the dining room, and when it came to bed time, he started to get agitated. I had told him he needed to stay in bed but he kept lying down on the floor with his face over the grate, talking to the Christmas tree.

It turned out we were in way over our heads with this child, and the evening quickly spiralled out of control. He could not stay in his room and kept denying he was out of it. He accused us all of lying and seemed to have a lot of anxiety about staying in the bedroom. I believe he was afraid of something happening, but I had not been given any info from Children's Aid. As we were the Emergency Shelter for the county, we knew we would receive undiagnosed children, but this kid needed immediate intervention from professionals.

He then started running around the house, out of control, yelling and screaming. It was late in the evening and we weren't qualified to deal with whatever was going on. I called Children's Aid and no one was available to come and get him, so they advised me to call the RCMP and have them pick him up for delivery to the hospital.

I placed the call but, unfortunately, we were also in the middle of a blizzard and it was going to be a while before a unit could get to us.

In the meantime, I had taken some medications he was on and placed them on the coffee table for when the police arrived. In one of his fly-by runs, he grabbed a bottle of pills and I reached out to try and grab them back, afraid of what he might do with them. He had a tight grip and twisted his hand, causing something to give way in my thumb but I got them back.

Then he escaped out into the night and both my husband and son were not far behind. He got as far as the poultry barns and managed to get hold of the wheelbarrow, which he pushed up the hill and frantically tried to ram through our stained-glass windows.

How could he manage this with two adult males in pursuit? He was fast and very agile. He could zig zag around reaching arms and duck grasping hands with ease.

But they did manage to catch him and I got a winter coat on him with some boots. I had frantically called the RCMP for their status and I know they weren't well pleased with getting this call, but somebody was going to get hurt if they didn't hurry.

My husband and son ended up pinning him between them, each with a tight hold on his arm and shoulder as they sat on the porch while the wind whipped stinging flakes into their faces. I couldn't risk trying to bring him inside. I wasn't sure how to position everyone to keep him secure.

He had become a mad man, kicking and screaming. What horrors had happened to him to reduce him to this?

The RCMP arrived, and the first officer out of the car came over, grabbed the boy and slung him over his shoulder like a sack of potatoes. He deposited Ryan in the back of the cruiser, and when they came over for some details, I mentioned I thought they had been kind of rough with him.

The officer calmly asserted, "When you've been kicked in the nuts as many times as I have, you don't take chances."

And that was that. Never heard any more about him or where he might have ended up. What resources would have been available to bring him into a world he had little experience with? Would it have been enough to overcome whatever horrors had represented the entirety of his life?

~

My next challenge was a very special young man of about ten years who came to us as another emergency placement. Some preliminary evaluations had been done and, for some reason, Kyle had been directed into the parent counsellor program. This was the same program Cynthia had been submitted to and allowed for very intense focus on behaviour and performance. I thought it a little heavy handed on the kids enrolled in the strict control and supervision.

Kyle would be with us a couple of weeks, and it was my privilege to get to know the beautiful person within.

Kyle was a talker and could converse nonstop for such extended periods of time, I wondered how his mouth didn't dry out. He had a habit of presenting odd bits of trivia from out of the blue and would quote sources if he was ever challenged.

He quickly exhausted the other kids in our home at the time and, although he was never offensive, I still noticed the others withdrawing from him and not being interested in spending any time with him. This was sad and, as we were told to put him in school for a brief couple of weeks, he had the same impact on the kids at school.

I can remember driving into town, with Kyle in the back seat rambling on in his usual way. I then caught him saying something that just made my heart sink.

"I have friends everywhere and I consider all the kids in my school friends even though they all said they didn't want to be my friend."

He wasn't put off by his declaration. He kept his head up, with chin firmly pointed forward, and I gave him credit for his persistence. How forgiving he was of those who rejected him. This defined Kyle, and I so wished we were in a different world that was more accepting of someone as cheerful and harmless as he was.

Kyle was with us when we decided to celebrate my son's birthday by going to a nice restaurant in Halifax. Looking back, I think it was a bad decision to include Kyle but, at the time, I wouldn't have considered leaving him behind. He was already excluded from so much; I didn't have the heart to tell him we're having a birthday party and you're not invited.

We arrived at the restaurant and we were all looking forward to a great meal and a birthday cake to follow. Kyle started up with his usual chatter, and I started to find it difficult to have a conversation with anyone that he didn't think wouldn't be improved by his commentary. I think he would have made a great politician, as no one would be able to get a word in edgewise.

Then I noticed the waitress was spending a lot of time hovering around Kyle. Not that she wanted to, but that he was finding a multitude of things that needed her attention. He wanted more ice in his glass, he needed another napkin, he wanted his own ketchup bottle, the breadsticks were getting low, etc.

"Kyle, she is not your persona slave," I reprimanded him. There was relief on the waitresses' face.

The food arrived and, as we occupied ourselves with eating, Kyle still managed to talk in between chewing food and gasping for air. The rest of us became more and more solemn as we gave up on our own prattle. Silently we were all of the same accord —let's just eat and get out of here.

The cake with burning candles was delivered to the boy who was cheering and clapping with so much excitement, unfortunately it wasn't my son. I had to correct the waitress and have it brought down to the real birthday boy, an easy error to make seeing as the cheer had left him at this point.

Kyle enjoyed himself immensely, and for that I am glad. I did however wonder if it would not have been better that, as a family, we should have some private moments to ourselves. I wanted so much to include the foster children in every aspect of our lives, but maybe I was arrogant in thinking we offered a glimpse into how a normal family lived.

Another day, I had a cat that required a visit to the vet and I decided to take Kyle with me to keep an eye on him. He enjoyed the drive, but I found the journey started to stress me out a bit as Kyle was being Kyle and, although noise didn't usually bother me, his voice was cutting through that insulated curtain around my brain.

At the clinic, the vet declined Kyle's diagnosis for my cat's issues and patiently answered his questions. Even the cat started to look a little frayed with the queries Kyle peppered throughout the consultation.

I found myself starting to worry about the return trip. Was there a shorter route that might get me home faster and cut short on the verbal onslaught? I thought there was a secondary road that should save me a few miles and I decided to give it a go.

Decisions should never be made in pre-panic mode.

We started off and the afternoon had become sweltering hot. I had no air conditioning and the cat started to yowl its contribution to the discomfort of the outing and maybe even Kyle's ongoing commentary.

I found the dirt road that would shave off a few minutes and bravely started down the dusty track. Without any cool air inside, the windows were down and now a steady haze of dust permeated the car.

"Did you know 80% of all men pee sitting down?"

I challenged this statement—I was pretty sure

most men delivered their urine from a standing position.

"Nope, I heard it on CKCL last September in their news."

I don't know where his ideas came from but it was important that he share his trivia with anyone and everyone.

I noticed there were no road signs. There should have been a marker and I was beginning to feel desperate.

"Dogs like squeaky toys because the sound makes them think they're killing something."

Good to know.

We had been driving over fifteen minutes on the dirt road and nothing in the surrounding geography looked familiar. We should have been climbing a mountain at this point but there was not a hill in sight. I had that sinking sensation you get when you realize you have made a big mistake.

"Did you know a dentist invented cotton candy?"

I was completely lost, and I had no other choice but to turn around and go back the way I had come. I had wasted fifteen minutes going in the wrong direction and would have to cover another fifteen minutes just to get back to my starting point and I was no closer to home.

At this point my mobile phone rang. It was my daughter calling to see what had happened and why I wasn't home yet.

I couldn't contain the panic in my voice. "I'm stuck in a hot car with a cat!"

Kyle was driving me crazy, but I was careful not to let him feel he might be the reason for my frustration. His brain was constantly spinning with true facts, and some not so true. He was like a big, wet sponge on a merry-go-round: anyone near was going to get soaked by the deluge of his wisdom. I was desperate to get home and find some relief from Kyle who cheerfully sat in the back seat and continued his revelations.

"You can't shoot pigs in Florida. They're a protected species."

It didn't matter if he was challenged about his statements. The sources for his information were just as fictional as his facts.

I eventually got on the right road and felt well-punished for the error of my ways, roadways to be exact. I got home and needed diversion anywhere that I couldn't hear Kyle.

Yet I felt guilty for needing that space and keeping him at a distance. His manner was always buoyant and sunny. He never had anything bad to say about anyone and I don't remember him complaining much.

Kyle was eventually moved forward to his parent counsellor's home and, once again, we were pressured to join the program and become parent counsellors ourselves.

It had no appeal to me, being so regimental in dealing with youth. Their restrictions and control may have been deemed necessary for some extreme cases, but the kids I saw diverted into the program didn't warrant the acute attention, in my opinion.

It was with great disappointment that Kyle ended back with us several months later and not because I wasn't glad to see him. His foster mother had struck him with a water bucket and Kyle was sent to us while the incident was investigated. He didn't understand why she had hit him and told me they were walking into a shed when she up and smacked him in the head with the big plastic jug. I bit my lip to avoid asking the question: *Were you talking at the time?*

A few days later Kyle was sent back to the same home and, several months after that, he was back in our care yet again and for the same reason. She hadn't used a water bucket, but had struck him and another time out was called for.

I don't know how she got away with it and why Kyle was again sent back to live with this family. Hitting him was bad enough, but what other abuse he might he be experiencing under her care and protection? How could Children's' Aid keep sending him back to someone who couldn't control themselves, especially someone who was supposed to be nurturing him? Was he feeling any tenderness or love?

Several years later, I was at a school assembly and was surprised to see Kyle walking by at a distance. He had grown up so big in those years, but there was something about his demeanour that disturbed me. His face was slightly twisted and his eyebrows were furrowed over hooded eyes.

As he got closer, he did not recognize me and I

could hear him talking to kids around him. He was being foul and obnoxious. Like a chained bear being poked for entertainment, he lashed out and threw nasty comments in every direction. It broke my heart to see him this way.

Gone was the cheerful, upbeat kid who considered everyone to be his friend. What had happened to him in those years to poison his spirit into the bitter, remorseless youth I now saw before me? Someone or something destroyed Kyle and would never be accountable for it. Who was there to save him from his rescuers?

~

Dylan was another guest in our home and came to us as respite for a permanent foster home in the area. He was a special needs child and had an unfortunate way of responding to the word "No". Whenever he heard that negative response to a request or question, he would immediately defecate in his pants.

The social worker let me know his situation well in advance just in case this might be one I declined to host. I hesitated a few seconds, and this was the first time I had ever needed to pause to mull it over.

I asked, "how bad can it be?" There has to be a limit to how often someone can soil themselves in the run of a day.

Five times was the answer. One day he had managed to foul himself five times in response to a no.

I really had to think about this one. I had never

turned away a child before and decided I wouldn't start now. It was proposed I would have Dylan one weekend every other month just to give his permanent Mom time to focus on other things as she was also home to a few other special needs children.

Dylan was brought to my home by his foster mom and she introduced us and reviewed his particular issues. His eyes were downcast, but when she got to the part where she described the problem he had with 'no', Dylan raised his eyes and probed mine. He was looking for my reaction and I tried to give him a reassuring smile.

I was also told that he would be responsible for cleaning himself and his clothes should an incident take place. This had been some conditioning in trying to get him to be responsible for his actions, and I thought it was terrific that he could look after himself that way.

I showed him around the house and let him know our basic rules. He still seemed a little nervous and when we went back downstairs, he was interested in the video games so I let him settle down in front of the TV screen.

I was in the middle of preparing supper so I left him with some of the other kids who did not know anything about his situation. This was a private thing not to be shared with anyone.

Supper was laid out on the table and I went into the living room to let everyone know. Dylan had been absorbed in an intense battle with one of the other kids and he was reluctant to shut it down.

"I want to play video games," was his blunt response to my invitation to supper. It took me moment to realize I was holding my breath.

I couldn't let him have his way just to avoid an incident and this would have been horrible timing, with him standing so close to the dining table. I decided to try something. I wouldn't say the actual word 'no' but my response would be negative nonetheless.

"You absolutely can play video games but I've just put supper on the table and I'd like you to have something to eat first."

Now it was his turn to consider my suggestion. I could see through his eyes that the brain was turning this over. Then without further discussion, he quietly put the controller down and took a place at the table. I was so relieved to have found this way of communicating without setting him off.

From then on, any time I needed to express a negative to his questions or requests, I said no without actually using the word 'no' and the entire weekend passed without any problems. I was happy and proud for us both, and I think Dylan also felt a sense of accomplishment. His foster mom picked him up later on Sunday and I had no problem telling her I would be happy to see him again anytime.

Another month passed and Dylan was with us for another weekend. There was a new foster child with us and they were immediately up for a challenge to play video games together. I retired to the kitchen to work on more meal prep but I froze when I heard something coming from the living room.

I tilted my head and slowly moved towards the kids and definitely heard "poopy" and "You're poopy." Something was happening and I walked into the room, steeling myself for what might meet me there. Both kids were well engaged in what they were doing and I heard it again.

"Poopy bum!" she hurled towards Dylan.

He seemed quite pleased to receive the insult. His personal issue had still never been discussed in front on anyone staying with us.

"Why are you calling him that?" I asked.

"Because he keeps beating me at Mario Kart!"

What a strange coincidence that she chose to use that form of teasing with a kid who had Dylan's unusual problem. They were enjoying themselves and no harm was intended or felt by either of them.

Dylan would continue to be an irregular visitor to the farm, and we never experienced any complications during his stays. I was so glad we were able to offer our home as respite to help out another foster family. For the kids, I hope they found our place welcoming and comfortable.

~

Steffanie was brought into our fold to give her some time to work out issues so challenging for a teenager. She was an amazing and sensitive girl with a beautiful personality and so intelligent. She had been diagnosed with bi-polar disorder and it was my first time seeing the effects up close and how disruptive this condition is to someone's day to day life. She was on medication and this may have smoothed down the edges but did not prevent the highs and lows from happening altogether.

We did our best to soften the intensity of her feelings of despair and mitigate the exaggerated sense of joy when episodes grabbed her. On top of everything a young person has to cope with, Steffanie had this additional complication to her life and it provided me an education into its hurtful effects.

I also have to give credit to the teachers at her junior high, who were much more familiar with coping with these situations. Steffanie told me one day that a teacher found her crying under the stairs and found her a quiet place where she could be undisturbed for as long as she needed to be. This kind of understanding was critical to helping her manage the mood swings and I was so glad she was treated with kindness and respect.

There was a lot about Steffanie to like. She was so considerate of others around her and she encouraged people to open up and be more accepting of themselves. She seemed so much more mature than most kids her age and always had this kind of Zen sensation that exuded through her very pores. I thought of her the way I think of artists who offer insights into themselves through their art. Steffanie laid bare her soul and didn't mask her emotions, so we all knew when she was having a hard time.

Steffanie was one of the kids I had to drive half

way to town to meet up with a school bus. One morning, I was getting things ready for everyone and realized she had overslept. We had to get up before anyone else because of her schedule, so no one was there when I hurriedly got her rolling.

Being late wasn't disastrous, but I found myself taking the opportunity during the car ride to lecture her on importance of respecting time. Work ethics and promptness were woven into my chastisement and she did her best to look attentive.

Half-closed eyes had me questioning if she had had a particularly bad night and as I started to question how much sleep she'd managed, I glanced at the dashboard clock. It showed I was exactly one hour ahead of what time it was supposed to be.

I had messed up the time and woken up an hour early and, in turn, had woken Steffanie up an hour early. She had calmly endured my pompous reprimand and I felt so guilty for dragging her out of bed.

As I started to apologize, I notice the corners of her mouth slowly crawling upwards. It was bad enough that she had been hauled out of bed so early but then to have to listen to my dribbling on and on about the challenges of a life that didn't respect punctuality? Steffanie was far more forgiving that I think I could have been.

I then told her that I owed her one and asked if there was something I could do to make it up to her. She thought about it a few minutes and then suggested something unusual. She told me she wanted to have lunch with me in town at a nice restaurant where we could have some one-on-one time. I was so flattered and surprised by her request.

I made sure we had our lunch without too much delay, and it was a really peaceful, relaxing opportunity to sit back and talk about nothing important. I was grateful for this chance and wish I had taken the time to do this sort of thing more often.

Steffanie had signed up for soccer that summer and she worked hard to practice and be physically fit. There were no guarantees and the team was building its player base from the submissions of kids from all around.

Whenever I took Steffanie to practice, several of the other kids would come with us and we followed her work outs attentively from the sidelines. Then came the day when final decisions would be made, and we were all sure Steffanie would be one of those chosen to carry on into the playing season.

All the hopefuls were on the field and going through their exercise. The coach approached individuals and said a few words, and they solemnly picked up their gear and left the grounds.

We collectively held our breath when he made his way towards Steffanie, hoping against hope he was offering some advice and not cutting her loose. We scrutinized her face from a distance, looking for indications that she was safe. She kept her composure and we were held ignorant until they turned away from each other and she started back towards us. We were all devastated and when she reached us, there was such an outpouring of sympathy and support.

I was really proud of how tightly our little group pulled together and tried to give her solace. Three weeks ago, some of us had never met, but to see us now would make you believe we had been closely bound for years.

We tried to assure her there would be another season and we were confident another opportunity would come her way.

Steffanie eventually returned to her family with more coping mechanisms in her tool belt and a very bright future ahead of her. We were so happy to have been a very brief part of her life.

~

Vicky was a teenager any adult would have been proud to call their own. She had a wicked sense of humour and displayed a radiant smile, free for all the world to see. She was a second pair of hands to me, helping out around the house and especially good with younger children. She was the kind of youth to guide a blind person across a street or help a complete stranger load their groceries.

While she was with us, Vicky volunteered at the local seniors' home and was so popular and helpful with staff and residents alike. She had been assigned to one lady who suffered from Alzheimer's and staff at the home were appreciative that Vicky could take her out for walks around the neighbourhood. She was just as useful to residents as she was to me at home, and I was so glad she shared so much of herself to others.

Vicky had trouble with her weight, in that she was too thin and sometimes made poor eating choices. I tried to combat this with what we had to offer, and we settled on something added to her diet that made us both happy.

She was on a kick at the time where she wanted to consume gelatin for her nails, and I offered to put a tablespoon of the stuff in a duck egg eggnog every morning before she left for school. The Muscovies that we were raising produced beautiful eggs with large yolks and it was no trouble to blitz up the drink and get some extra calories into her.

The eggnogs were absolutely delicious and some of the other kids thought they were missing out on something, so I sometimes had orders for several eggnogs in the morning—minus the gelatin.

Vicky's determination to help sometimes put her at risk. One night, as we were coming home from town, I hit a deer that jumped out in front of the car. As soon as I pulled over, Vicky was quick to jump out of the car, with me scrambling after her, yelling at her to stay away. If it was still alive, it might be kicking and the hooves could be sharp.

We weren't much comfort to the deer, but its injuries weren't that serious as it jumped up and ran away.

Another day we were on a trip to a beach when we saw smoke ahead of us. It turned out to be a barn fire, and although no animals were in the barn, several horses were in the corral and had become quite spooked by the developing blaze.

I shouldn't have even stopped the car, as there were already people there and no one needed our help, but again, Vicky was gone like a shot. I was so afraid for her and although I screamed at her to stay out of the corral, I didn't think she would have listened to me.

When I caught up to her, I was relieved to find she had stayed out of the pen but was hanging over the top rail of the corral and had a horse by its bridle, trying to calm it down. She was definitely the type of person who would have dived into a burning building to save someone.

Vicky enjoyed the wildlife at our farm, even down to the starlings that nested in the eaves of the carriage shed. When spring produced the first batch of fledglings, she was determined to teach them something.

She had heard they were good at mimicry and she started to wolf whistle whenever she passed by the shed. Sure enough, by the fall there were several birds giving her the whistle exactly as she had taught them that spring. She would step out onto the porch and return their raucous call, much to her own amusement.

~

An unexpected guest to our home was a two-month-old baby. We were not set up for infants and I had requested we not take in any babies, but this was an emergency and the usual infant foster homes were not available.

I was promised we would have him no more than a week. I eventually would learn that this was code for anywhere from two to six months.

Children's Aid gathered some furniture and delivered it and little Cameron to us. I set up a temporary nursery in a room at the top of the stairs and our teen girls immediately started to compete for the chance to play with a baby. I found myself pushed to the side and, as long as I made sure diapers were changed and bottles made ready, I seemed to be excluded from caring for him.

The one thing the girls were not comfortable doing was giving the baby a bath and, it turned out, neither was Cameron. I was familiar with the kicking and splashing raucous adventure that usually left me soaked, but I was surprised when I lowered Cameron into the tub and he immediately stiffened up. His eyes were wide and darted around, unsure of what was happening. Until that moment, I didn't realize he had never had a bath.

I tried dribbling warm water over his belly, splashing some on his legs and arms, and he still hadn't made up his mind whether this was a good thing or a bad thing. The biggest tell was that he was silent through the entire procedure. Cameron was constantly laughing and giggling, but he was restrained and just not sure how to interpret the experience.

It wasn't until the second or third bath that he

started to get into it and produce the jerky kicks that could scatter the contents of his tub all over my kitchen. Babies love bath time, and Cameron was no different once he was introduced. The wood stove in the kitchen made it a warm, cozy place to give him his daily bath, and it became a ritual that was exciting for us both.

Cameron was in need of shots, and Children's Aid asked me to arrange them with a local doctor. It was somewhat urgent, as he had missed his first boosters and needed to get started with the schedule they usually like to follow when lining up the various needles.

I called the doctor's office and pressed for the receptionist to squeeze us in for a quick visit. When I arrived, I was given a stern lecture on the importance of keeping up with the shots according to the timing always in place and how I shouldn't expect everyone to drop what they're doing to accommodate my delinquency.

I looked around the waiting room and saw several faces united in support of the receptionist's reprimand. Mouths were tightened in silent conviction and the occasional eyebrow was raised presenting a mild challenge.

It was embarrassing, but I explained how I was a foster parent and this baby had been taken into emergency care and we were in a hurry to see he got the care and attention that had so far been forsaken.

Now it was her turn to be embarrassed. She was focusing on straightening out her desk and couldn't look up to meet my eyes. With a slight stutter, she guided me into an examination room to await the doctor and left Cameron and me to our own devices.

I didn't know how long we would be there, so I laid Cameron out on the examination table and loosened his blankets. Cameron was always quick to smile and I started blowing farts on his belly, which sent him into waves of laughter.

There is something infectious about a baby's laugh and I found myself responding with my own chuckles and giggles. In this way, it didn't seem long before the doctor was there and happily gave Cameron a once-over before giving him the needles.

Cameron was briefly upset, but wasn't long getting back to his cheerful temperament, and as we came out of the waiting room, there were quite a few smiling faces. A pleasant turnaround from when we first arrived.

We only had Cameron with us less than two months, but that time was filled with joy, as we all competed to spend time with him.

Before he left us, I had opportunity to visit the offices of Children's Aid and was ambushed yet again by a social worker, who wanted me to meet Cameron's parents. This was so awkward for me, as I was aware of the neglect that had brought him into care, but I had to bury any attitude I might have and engage in some pleasant chit-chat with his parents.

I was brought into a room for some privacy with them, and was surprised at how young they were. His mother didn't look any more than 17 and the father not much older. They were still kids them-selves, and probably didn't know the first thing on how to look after a baby.

I made remarks about Cameron's cheerful dispos-ition, how big he was and how they must be so proud of their baby, and so on. They seemed so happy to hear how he was doing and couldn't stop thanking me for looking after him.

Their gratitude made me so uncomfortable, and I don't know why.

Cameron was eventually placed with a foster fam-ily I was quite familiar with and knew he would be in good hands.

I managed to meet up with his new foster mom a few months later, and she commented on how Cameron was definitely used to a lot of attention. She was grinding her teeth a little as she said this, so I'm not sure it was intended as any kind of praise for what we had accomplished with him. Maybe she didn't have enough teenage girls in her home.

Further down the road, Cameron was returned to his home, with his parents receiving all the support Children's Aid could offer.

~

Children's Aid did keep us busy and with few excep-tions, our home was improved by their presence. We learned so much from them and I hope we made a difference to a few of them. We were a brief resting spot for many children on their own journey. Victims of circumstance and challenging environments, their resilience and strength served them well.

For my part, I felt it my obligation to keep them busy and occupied, but on one occasion I over-stepped the mark. In my attempts to keep our teens active and entertained, I made the mistake of organizing a ghost-hunting expedition.

There was a house down towards Five Islands that had a long-standing reputation for ghost sightings. I have to confess to encouraging the kids to do something that was technically illegal. The property was privately owned and, although abandoned for many years, it still belonged to someone who had not invited us to explore its cracks and crannies.

I packed up four teens and headed out after dark, making sure everyone had a flashlight and nerves of steel. It took almost an hour to get there and, one of the kids with us knew the location and history of the house.

Once we got there, I had to drive by slowly a few times to make sure there was no one around to see us. There were occupied houses not far down the road and I suggested we not use the flashlights until we got into the house. There was a driveway but it had long been overgrown and I was forced to leave my car on the side of the road.

The house loomed towards us out of the darkness, casting an outline that gave credibility to the spooky stories of shapes and shadows permeating its structure. A large porch skirted the two-story wood frame building, with half of the roof drunkenly leaning towards the ground. This introduction was the prelude to a very tired, fragile structure presenting warped, loose boards under our feet.

The interior was exactly as one would imagine. Broken window panes allowed a slight breeze to flutter the remains of faded wallpaper weakly clinging to crumbling plaster. Our feet took measured steps, testing each board before transferring our full weight forward.

An open door tilted on rusty hinges discouraged our entrance as we gathered at the bottom of a wide set of stairs. We were enveloped by dank, mouldy air as flashlights now exposed corners and doorways.

The teens were excited and determined to investigate every nook and cranny. It was decided they would work in teams while I stayed at the entrance and watched for trouble.

To say they were over-stimulated is an understatement. They weren't long interpreting the simplest of objects into something sinister and menacing. The upstairs team found a pair of ladies red shoes at the top of the stairs, sitting side by side, ready for an occupant. They developed a story in which the woman of the house was trying to escape an abusive husband, but before she could get the shoes on, she was murdered and her body hidden somewhere on the property. No such event had ever taken place but in their minds, it was feasible.

Downstairs team browsed the kitchen and brought me a butter knife from the kitchen, along with their own unlikely tale of gore and savagery.

This was the knife that was used to torture farm animals and wandering salesmen who had the misfortune to visit the property.

My suggestion that they needed to pull it back a little didn't get much of a foothold. I insisted they return the knife and that no one was allowed to take anything from the property.

Upstairs team came down to join the others and together they explored a few more rooms. They were doing a great job of frightening each other and were convinced at one point that they had seen a shadow cross a doorway when no one was in the room. They created a few incidents of ghostly phenomena to justify the alarm radiating from every pore of their bodies.

I think it was actually a relief when we were suddenly accosted by an elderly man, yelling at us to get out and leave the property. He was quite angry

Apparently, the house often received unwanted guests. He had appointed himself guardian and I don't blame him for giving us the boot. We, along with everyone else visiting the house, were a nuisance to this community and someday, someone stupid was going to light a match and send it all up in flames. We hurried back through the overgrown grass and shrubs and left without any argument.

As we settled in to the long drive home, the teens shared more of what they thought they saw or heard and their experiences evolved into the unexplainable. I pushed reasonable explanations for so much of what they thought happened, but I think they were so much happier thinking they had experienced something truly paranormal.

This outing had ignited way too much excitement and they were already talking about where the next ghost hunt should take place. It was disappointing to them when I told them there would be no more ghost trips.

I used their current state of mind as a good reason why we could never do it again, and they feigned outrage. I tried to point out they had become overstimulated and had imagined a lot of what they thought had happened. This wasn't healthy.

The teens insisted the outing had not upset or disturbed them in any way. They tried to convince me they had not found the experience disturbing and that it brought them some desperately-needed excitement. After all, people were paying to go on ghost tours in Halifax, so how upsetting could it possibly be?

The answer to that question came the next morning when I got up and found every light in the house on. No one would admit to turning the lights on, but I was pretty sure it was one of the 'unaffected' kids struggling to deal with the dark.

This went on for the next three days, with everyone denying responsibility for turning on the lights in every room of the house. Then I found out one of the kids had taken the butter knife away with them. I made them take it out to the field and bury it.

I needed the event to be over and done with so we could return to our normal state of looking after as many kids as Children's Aid would send us.

~

There was a small family of three children whose mother had a bit of a breakdown. They were with us because no family or friends were available to take them. A few days later the mother had gathered herself and resources assigned to help her cope with the long term.

It had been a disruption for the children to be plucked out of their familiar living situation and dropped suddenly into a place they didn't know with people they had never met. The oldest child had been in the middle of a sporting tournament and was doing well with his team, but Children's Aid were not able to provide transport to the competition for him. He was very frustrated by missing his play-offs and a little less concerned about his mother, but they were not with us long and soon the family was reunited.

~

One of the most tragic cases I remember was that of a 12-year-old boy who was well-known in the system and brought out to us as part of an ongoing and seemingly never-ending attempt to adapt him to home living.

James was often found wandering the streets of Truro, using survival skills that would have been impressive if they weren't so sad. His father was not in the picture and he often spent time with his mother, but home life was fractured and left him living independently of any adult supervision. He had a good relationship with his mom but she didn't seem to have any concerns about where he was or what he was doing any time day or night.

I have to give James's credit for how he adapted to this world. He might have been frequently on his own, but many people knew him and had no problem offering him what he needed. He knew if he was hungry, he could go to the kitchen in the hospital and they would feed him. He knew where it was safe to sleep without being disturbed or attacked.

I didn't really understand why he didn't go home where he had a bed, but negligence had caused him to develop his own rhythm. Although James didn't seem to need anyone, Children's Aid worked hard to offer him a safe, secure alternative but he was not comfortable staying in one place.

When he was delivered to us, he immediately started pacing back and forth, insisting he couldn't live in the country because he was used to city life. Truro was not, in my definition, a city, but it was the stomping grounds he had accustomed himself to and a farm was a foreign and frightening place.

James managed to stay with us three short days, and he let me know he was leaving before he took off. I desperately tried to persuade him to stay, but he couldn't handle the openness of the fields and the lack of people.

I gave him some stuff to take with him and told him I would be calling the RCMP as part of my safety requirements. I told him how to get to town and that the RCMP would pick him up and take him where he wanted to go.

He wasn't the first kid who had chosen to leave us, and I was comfortable knowing he wouldn't be out there long. The police let me know when they had him in their care, and what happened after that was up to Children's Aid.

~

Not every kid flourished in our care, but for the every one we couldn't help, there were so many we could. I appreciated having had the opportunity to share my life with so many wonderful kids. It is an experience I would recommend to anyone thinking of bringing a child into their home.

Children's Aid offers a lot of support to foster parents and the process involved in orientation will let you know if this is something for you. Check out the section "Becoming a foster parent", at the back of the book.

10: All creatures great and small

Our farm was located on 120 acres of land that was slowly returning to a natural woodland, hosting a healthy variety of wildlife around and amongst us. We had become integrated into the living beauty that surrounded us and to descend our driveway was like stepping through a portal to another world. Creatures of all sizes shared the fields and forests with us and they contributed to an overall sense of oneness with nature.

We became familiar with several of our four-legged neighbours who carried on about their business as indifferent to us as if we were part of the scenery. It was that acceptance of our presence that made us feel privileged to be there, sharing this space and making us wardens of the fields and forests.

One of our most memorable neighbours was a skunk who lived under the abandoned dairy barn. It liked to forage casually around the house, digging for grubs and, when the mood would strike him, taking naps under our porch. This was a south facing veranda and also the choice location the girls had picked out for sunbathing.

Neither party was willing to give up their spot so, if you didn't mind the pungent smell so much, you could still get a pretty good tan. If your positioning allowed it, you could even peek through the weather-stained boards and be eye to eye with the drooping eyelids of the skunk no more than 18 inches below where you lay.

I've always admired how nonchalant skunks are in interactions with humans. As long as we don't irritate them, they just do their thing and ignore us. Having a nap under the boards of our porch with a teen laid out on top was no different.

We were on our way back from town one day and came across a mother skunk with almost half a dozen babies on the side of the road. I'm unsure of the number because the little balls of black and white fur were a tight sphere that continuously rolled as they crawled over and under each other. It almost looked like a pot boiling on the stove, but once in a while, one of them would break free and make a dash for our truck. The others followed suit, creating the appearance of a conga line, but we would hear the mother chirp and they would pull back to her side and continue their black-and-white imitation of a pot boiling over.

There is nothing cuter that a baby skunk! I've heard they make amazing pets and I don't know if I could have said no if we were lucky enough to find one abandoned.

Our own menagerie consisted of two cats, both long hairs with one an orange tabby cat and the other a calico Manx. The older cat, Cricket, was not that active and of no threat to mice or birds in and around the house. We even had a bird feeder in the back and, encouraged by the flurry of hungry birds, he would sometimes sit under the feeder, waiting for an incredibly stupid bird to fly into his mouth.

As it was, the birds had a sense that there was nothing to fear from this cat and disrespectfully hopped around on the ground as close as two feet from him. Cricket would watch but made no moves and could have been a lawn ornament for all the menace he presented to them. I'm not sure he thought the exertion of pouncing would have been worth the small snack a bird provided. His feline instincts were still intact, even though he made no effort to launch an attack.

Cricket did have some unusual taste buds and was a connoisseur of all foods. If something was good enough for you, it was good enough for him, and this extended to whatever the ducks and guineas might eat. We often tore up old bread and busted muffins we got from the food bank to feed our poultry, and it was always a sight to see Cricket deep amongst the flock, gobbling down the tasty treats our birds enjoyed so much. They seemed to accept him as one of the flock, but it was still a little unnerving to see him head down, pecking at the food alongside his feathered friends.

I got the feeling the other birds, wild and domestic, considered him 'special' and simply accepted his presence amongst them.

Our little calico Manx was very good at controlling the mice around our old farm house and, sadly, she also targeted the hummingbirds that hung around our flowering shrubs. I would often open our front door in the morning and find an offering of one these little creatures on the step and, even though we put a bell on her collar, she was still able to get a hold of them.

We had no idea just how many mice she was getting until, one day, we had to move the truck and found a mouse graveyard scattered underneath it. The entire space protected by the truck was peppered with dead, headless mice and could have made for horror movie material.

Why she left the bodies untouched was a mystery, but she was definitely a prolific mouser.

Leading out from our huge kitchen was a back door that opened into a small landing with a back staircase, and a further door that allowed access to our wood room. My husband went back there one day, and when he opened the wood room door, a mouse was desperately grasping the door frame five feet from the floor and was frantically waddling his way down. He was putting so much effort into not losing his grip that my husband stood watching him until he reached the floor and took off for the kitchen wood pile.

Both cats were sitting in front of their food dishes, which also happened to be in front of the wood pile, and the introduction of a mouse was not lost on our PB. She saw him dive in and was immediately in pursuit, poking and pawing around the sticks until she harassed the mouse into seeking another asylum.

He exited the wood pile and dove under Cricket, who had been watching the hunt with disinterest and even a little boredom.

PB knew the mouse had escaped but wasn't quite sure where he had gone. The mouse had found refuge under Cricket's thick orange fur and wasn't moving. As with the birds around the bird feeder, the mouse must have sensed that hiding under this big orange cat was the safest place to be.

PB, on the other hand, had become frantic trying to locate the mouse. When Cricket finally stood up, there was the mouse frozen in place for all to see.

PB immediately pounced, swatting the mouse back towards the door, where he quickly escaped into the back-room wood pile and beyond reach of a very disappointed cat. We didn't know it then, but we would meet this mouse again later that summer.

One morning, as I stepped out on our front porch, I was greeted with the delightful sight of several deer munching the grass beside our garage. We had a couple of cords of hardwood stacked neatly in rows nearby and my attention was drawn to PB, who was crouched on top.

A little fawn scampered over to the pile and PB dove down behind the stacks for just a few seconds before she jumped back up in surprise attack mode. The fawn hopped away a few feet and our cat again crouched on top of the hardwood castle with ears flattened, ready to spring.

The fawn then charged the woodpile with all the menace of a butterfly and our cat dove back down behind the woodpile. This went on for several minutes.

I had never seen two different species play with each other like that before. It was captivating and I could have stood there all day, but the fawn was eventually called away when its mother moved down towards the orchard for some better grazing.

Disappointed, PB sat on top of the logs and waited for the fawn to return, but it wasn't to happen that day.

It was by this time that my husband convinced Shane that they should try to raise some pigeons and see if they could train them to do something. A lot of them had been seen entering and leaving the old barn, so one day, the two of them went on their mission to retrieve a baby from a nest.

They marched down into the barn with a ladder clasped under their arms and I had some concerns about the lack of planning they had invested. They weren't long coming back up the hill and I was presented the trophy of one kidnapped pigeon chick.

Not familiar with raising a small bird like this, I took a guess and tried it out on a diet of crushed up Cheerios and dry kibble from our cats, mixed with water into a paste. I then used the narrow end of an espresso spoon to feed the perpetually-hungry little creature, and kept it bundled up in the pocket of a shirt I wore.

I carried this bird with me everywhere I went, and it was beside me when I went to bed at night.

The little bird was doing well, but as more of its feathers started to grow in, I began to wonder what it actually might be. The plumage was dark, charcoal grey and it had a flamboyant yellow beak.

When I drew this to my husband's attention, I asked what other birds were nesting in the barn. He had noticed some starlings flapping around but didn't think they were actually nesting there. Starlings are opportunists and would happily have set up a colony in the spacious and protective barn.

So now we realized that I was raising a starling, a bird I had never admired. I myself thought of them more like a flying rat. They travelled in gangs, loudly pronouncing their uninvited presence as they surged across lawns and parking lots, looking for scraps.

I didn't like starlings and now one was peering up at me with glassy black eyes, blinking innocently as he anticipating his next snack. It wasn't his fault he had been plucked from the security of his nest and plopped into my care.

I set my personal opinion aside and made a commitment to raise him as best I could, and eventually try to introduce him back to his outdoor friends.

There is a feeling that develops when you realize something is dependent on you for its very being, and my protective nature was kicking in for this helpless little creature.

We named the little starling Shadow, and it wasn't

long before he had his full plumage and I started exercising his wings. He would be perched on my hand and I would quickly drop my hand down, making him think he had lost his roost, causing him to flap frantically.

I would do this several times a day and, just by the feel of his weight on my finger, I knew he was getting stronger, till he could actually be airborne on his own for several seconds.

This progressed till I was tossing him a few feet to the back of a chair and he was soon in control of the airways. Our cats had to be put outside during the day until night time, when Shadow would be put in a cage.

He spent a lot of time on my shoulder, pecking at my earrings, and he had a bad habit of sometimes trying to poke my eyeball. He was very attached to me and I became very attached to him.

Shadow spent a lot of time sitting in the window singing to other birds, and I always felt quite sad for him at these times. He should have been left in his nest and not interfered with, but for as long as we had him, he was a part of the family and would often take naps on a vacant shoulder or ankle.

I had a large jade plant in one of the windows and he loved to sit there and have staring contests through the glass with PB, who was frustrated at not being allowed inside during the day.

While sitting in the plant, he sometimes made a mess and I went in search of an old toothbrush to keep my window sill clean. I found one way up top of the medicine cabinet, tucked in behind some toiletries, and I went to work periodically scrubbing away the droppings. I always returned the toothbrush to its spot so no one would accidentally use it.

Then came the day when my husband came stomping into the kitchen. "Who's been using my toothbrush?"

"What do you mean using your toothbrush?" I started to get a sinking sensation in my stomach.

"My toothbrush is wet—someone's been using it."

"Where have you been keeping it?"

"I keep it way up behind some stuff in the medicine cabinet so no one would find it and use it."

My husband had a paranoia that someone would use his personal things, so he tucked away anything he didn't want the risk of sharing. It's only been 30 years and this incident is still a sore point in our marriage. I think it was his own fault for hiding the toothbrush in the first place.

He has since used the event to justify securing things from me and I am unrepentant. He feels violated and I still won't justify his wariness in tucking personal effects secretively around the house. For now, just mention the word 'toothbrush' and he is immediately triggered into telling his story again and again.

Shadow made it difficult for me to leave the house by clinging to the top of my head. I didn't think he was quite ready for the outdoors, but whenever I approached a door to leave, he tried to burrow into my hair and go with me. I would reach up and grasp him tightly before pitching him with force toward the far end of the living room. To an observer, it would appear I was trying to throw a ball to a player. He always spread his wings, swooped into a graceful pivot and was well on his way back to me as I tried to slip through the door and shut it before he could regain his perch on my head.

One day I left him in this manner, and when I got home from town, my husband met me in the yard. While I was gone, one of the kids had left the door open and PB had slipped in, quickly putting an end to Shadow.

I cried over that silly little bird, something I never wanted but fell in love with despite my misgivings.

I look at all starlings differently now. I see them as handsome, graceful and intelligent survivors and often wish I had another Shadow, but we'll never disturb a nest again. It's funny how my perspective did a 180 after caring for that beautiful little creature.

The first spring after opening our home to foster children, we picked up a load of turkey chicks and brought them back to raise for meat. They were cared for in the back room off the kitchen where the secondary stairwell was, and we attached a nice heat lamp to their box to keep them warm and cozy.

While I was looking after them, it became apparent that one of the birds was having trouble standing up. One leg didn't seem to want to support its weight and I started taking some time each day to work the weaker leg and give it some exercise to strengthen it.

This seemed to help but it wasn't thriving like the

other birds, and when it was time to move them to the poultry barn, I wondered if it was going to survive.

Kimberly couldn't stand the idea that it might be bullied by the now bigger siblings and begged for me to let it stay in her room until the leg improved enough to reintroduce back into its little flock. I reluctantly agreed and a nest was set up in her room, where she could look after it and continue working on the weak leg. She took her turkey everywhere except school, and within a few weeks, it was well enough to go to the barn.

Kimberly would have happily kept the turkey until it was full grown and had it as a permanent pet, but that was a definite no on my part.

Even after it was relocated and putting on lots of weight, Kimberly used to visit it, and it would attempt to jump into her lap like it used to do as a chick but now it weighed 14 or 15 pounds. This usually knocked her back on her butt. The bird had no idea it was so much bigger. It still thought he could cuddle up into her neck and be rocked in the crook of her arm.

In an effort to involve the foster children in the workings of our poultry farm, I decided the next spring to take the kids with me when we picked up our turkey chicks for that year. They would all be allowed to pick out a bird that would be theirs to give to their family when Thanksgiving rolled around. I sent them off with one of the staff while I wandered the store, picking up feed and so forth.

Then, while I was standing in line to pay for everything, I overheard one of the employees talking to another.

"There's a bunch of kids down there trying to pick out the sickest looking birds!"

This got my attention—it was obviously my kids he was talking about. Why were they looking for sick turkeys? Then it hit me, Kimberly had been allowed to keep a turkey in her room because it had something wrong with it. In their minds, if they had a sick or injured bird, they might get to keep it in their rooms as well.

I had four kids looking at turkeys and there was no way my home would become hospice to ill or wounded birds. The smell and the mess would have been out of this world and would have made for a bizarre environment. They hadn't included me in this plan so it would have been a surprise to get home and realize we had a minor plague infecting only their birds.

They were optimistic that they might be able to convert them to pets but, luckily, none of the birds had any issues. There was nothing stopping the kids from being attentive to their wards, so they had to resign themselves to spending time with them in the poultry barn, not their bedrooms.

I can just imagine Children's Aid getting wind that I was allowing the kids to take a live turkey to bed with them. It would not have gone well.

I did allow some kids to have pets, but only the long-term foster children, not the emergency intake ones. Kimberly made the decision that she wanted a rat, and it was under the conditions that she not only be the caregiver of her pet but that, should something come up, she would also be responsible for veterinarian costs.

Kimberly was working part time and had no problem with the rules, so she picked out an albino rat which she named Athena, Greek goddess of war.

I thought rats were an unusual pet, but Athena proved to be a very curious and intelligent rat. Kimberly paid her a lot of attention and took her everywhere and there was a lot of affection shared between the two of them.

It was unfortunate that Athena became ill and needed a visit to the vet, who diagnosed her with pneumonia. The small bedroom off the dining room was unoccupied at the time, so we set it up as a sick room for Athena. I even had a humidifier in the room and we kept the door shut to prevent drafts. Her breathing was quite laboured and we made sure she had a comfortable pillow to lie on.

It was difficult to watch her deteriorate despite our following the vet's recommendations. Kimberly started sleeping in the room with Athena, but the next day had to go to work.

I was standing in the doorway as Kimberly left and saw the rat trying to crawl after her, and I realized that Athena didn't want to be left alone. I think she was scared and knew something was wrong with her.

We set up a schedule with anyone willing to take

shifts keeping Athena company, and this seemed to reduce her stress. The following day, Kimberly was off at work again when I happened to be taking a shift with Athena. She was cuddled under my chin when I felt her body jerk and I knew something was up.

When I rolled her onto her back, I could see she had stopped breathing. I tried manipulating her chest for a while but it was no good. Athena, goddess of war had lost the battle and passed away. I was so glad someone was with her when she died.

When Kimberly got home that day, I broke the news to her. She had anticipated it happening and had already come to terms with Athena's passing.

High up on Nuttby Mountain, on the way to where I usually met the school bus for the kids attending in town, there was a scenic, abandoned, old farm house that locals and strangers alike often photographed. It stood in isolation, with a slight tilt that portrayed the image of a fragile building on the verge of collapse. Protruding from the ground surrounded by vacant fields, grey boards clung tenuously to old studs and empty windows yawned sleepily, swallowing strong winds that threatened to give the house that final push. The house had resisted nature's attempts to level its structure and represented a deceptive strength that had kept it upright for many years.

It was here that Kimberly decided she wanted to bury Athena. As the house had stood strong and un-changed for so many years, Kimberly thought it would be a safe resting place for her precious friend.

Everyone who was with us at that time went with Kimberly and shared her heartbreak as she dug a little hole near the foundation. With Athena tenderly wrapped up and placed in a cookie tin, she committed her to the ground and many of us cried when Kimberly spoke of how much Athena had meant to her.

It seemed to me for the first time that the attachment foster kids make with an animal is so important to them. For whatever reason, someone who has lost connection with their family might find solace in a pet. I couldn't make this possible for the temporary kids in our care, but I encouraged long-term children to consider taking on a pet.

One of the most interesting encounters with wildlife in our area took place high in the skies over our head.

Years ago, my brother had gifted us a huge kite. I can't remember the dimensions exactly, but I think it could have doubled as a small tent. In an effort to avert the threat of boredom, we gave it to Shane to try his luck out in the fields around our house. He had no problem getting the kite up in the air and, because it had a long string, it was really gaining some altitude.

In Shane's first flight, it was a surprise to see a large eagle appear and take its time circling the kite. A curiosity for sure, and did he see the kite as an invader?

After several minutes of checking things out, the eagle melted back into the scenery.

A couple of the kids had an opportunity to hold the cord, and it was natural for them to let out more and more of its length. At the rate they were going, it was soon going to need an aviation obstacle light.

Then came the hard part—reeling the string back in as the kite was slowly pulled back to earth. This was the not-so-fun part and Wade and Shane ended up taking turns as muscles complained about the repetitive motions of rolling the wooden stick.

Wade is someone who likes to tinker with mechanical things, and he decided he had to develop something that would pull the kite in automatically. It was designed to do all the rolling and save the strain on the wrists and arms of anyone who might want to play with the kite.

What he came up with would have looked at home in a steampunk art exhibit. Ugly, with motor parts scavenged from some household device, it required a 12-volt motor to power it. It wasn't fast, but it did the job and, as long as you didn't let the cord build up in one spot on the roller, it was smooth sailing.

In subsequent excursions, the eagle would quietly appear high above, sharing the skies with the kite every time it went up. I often wondered if it would attack the intruder, but it never did. It kept peace with the strange object penetrating in its territory.

There were other encounters with animals around the farm and we became familiar with a beautiful male fox whom the kids named Tri-pod. He ran using three legs and when he slowed to walk, he limped, putting little weight on that fourth leg. It's possible he had injured his foot in a snare, but otherwise he seemed quite healthy.

One sunny afternoon in February, I watched from a distance as two foxes emerged from the tree line and made their way across the expansive field in front of me. There was no snow on the ground but their coppery orange fur was still in contrast to the beige background of flattened dead grass.

It was Tri-pod and an unknown little female who was behaving like an energetic puppy, grabbing leaves and throwing them in the air as she ran circles around him.

His pace did not waver, even with his limp, and I watched them make their way as two lovers oblivious to the world. The female looked so elated to be with him, a wide smile accentuated by her black gums declared her joy for all to see. Tri-pod on the other hand contained his excitement and didn't falter as he kept his pace and, within too short a time, was out of my sight.

I had never seen this kind of display before, and when I called my father that night, he told me February was mating season for foxes in preparation for kits to be born in April. I felt I had been privileged to see something so intimate between two wild creatures. It was one of many bonuses of being on our farm.

There were other occasions when I think the wildlife took us for granted. One night, my husband had to respond to a nature call of his own and, while in the bathroom, heard a scratching at the door. Thinking it must be one of our cats, he opened the door to see a mouse sitting in the middle of the doorway. It looked up at him and hobbled over under our green swivel rocker and turned to watch him.

My husband shut and door and returned to his duty when again came the scratching at the door. Again, he opened the door and the same mouse was sitting there looking up at him, except this time he didn't turn to hide under the chair.

My husband took this as his cue to step aside and keep the entrance clear and, with that, the mouse limped past him to the vanity where it disappeared down the side of a pipe into the basement.

Because of the injury to his hind leg, we took it that this might be the mouse PB had smacked a few months back when it had hidden under Cricket in the kitchen. I thought it a little brazen of it to sit and wait for my husband to move out of the way before continuing on its route. It could at least have pretended to be afraid, but, as with the birds when Cricket sat under the bird feeder, he must have had a sense that he was in no danger here.

Animals recognized Wade as a friend, and often, when we visited a home with pets, he would walk into a room and, as soon as he crouched, cats or dogs would instantly make their way over to him looking for ear scratches and belly rubs. No word was spoken but there was a communication nonetheless. They sensed his gentle nature and affection for all creatures.

Fall was a dangerous season for me when driving with Wade. Every time a leaf skipped across the road ahead of our headlights, he would hit the brakes, thinking it might be a frog or toad. I almost felt the need for a neck brace to protect myself from the frequent jerking back and forth on a windy night.

Another dangerous activity was the seemingly-innocent act of hanging up laundry to dry. Not far from the spot we stood to pin clothes on the line, I had hung a hummingbird feeder, and these little spitfires were quite territorial. I often had to soothe frightened girls when the birds zoomed in to within inches of their faces, hovering on invisible wings and threatening to advance. They knew how to intimidate despite their size, and it was necessary to assure the girls that no one had ever been attacked by a hummingbird.

Deer were a familiar sight in the fields around us, and they had taken a liking to many items in our gardens, but there was one deer in particular I had heard about but never set eyes on. He was a big buck and fittingly called 'The Ghost'. Every fall, hunters geared up and permeated our woodlands searching for the elusive creature, determined to possess this trophy for themselves.

I had just seen the kids off to school on a chilly October morning with a light skiff of snow covered the ground. Then something caught my eye and I saw a deer step out from behind our garage and move upwards across our driveway. It was the infamous

Ghost, and his rack was indeed a splendour to behold. He was dragging his right front leg ever so slightly, but he was huge and looked to be in fantastic shape.

Excitedly, I called my father who lived in the valley about two hours distance from us. I provided him a vivid description and teased him about grabbing his guns and getting up here. I reminded him that hunters had been looking for the ghost for years but, despite the competition, he had survived every year with survival skills of his own.

I had finished teasing him, and asked what he thought about it.

He responded with what I thought was a silly question: "Who were you looking to talk to?"

"Dad?"

"No."

I had apparently called a wrong number, and the man hadn't even tried to interrupted me as I went on about this mysterious buck.

I apologized profusely for bothering him with all this nonsense and he was gracious, but as I said goodbye and moved to place the receiver back unto the cradle, I could hear him suddenly shout, "Wait a minute! Where do you live?!"

Too late—I had already hung up and, whoever he was, he was at least one less hunter looking for the Ghost.

Sightings for the Ghost continued a few more years, and I never heard of anyone claiming him for their own. I really did hope he managed to evade the hunters and, according to the sportsmen in my family, deer had been conditioned over the years to head deeper into the woods during hunting season.

Whether this is true or not I can't say, but one of the deer's habits was to 'yard up' in the fall into huge herds. I counted 23 does in a pasture not far from our farm one late October, so the numbers were pretty good.

Every spring the grouse continued his display for us at the top of the driveway, Tri-pod often crossed the decrepit pastures in full view of the farm house and sometimes, late at night, the kids would go out and chase deer around the meadows.

The kids put up a tent one night down past the gardens, and the next morning wanted to know who was trying to scare them by sniffing around. There was a black bear in the area and we were not sure if he had been inspecting, but the kids moved the tent right in front of the house.

I enjoyed sharing the farm's territory with all the animals that made it their home in the fields and forests around us. We were just passing through, and it was all the creatures surrounding us that willingly shared their abode. This never belonged to us and it's a bad habit of ours that we try to possess things that give us pleasure. I'm so grateful to have experienced the farm and, like a beautiful sunset, we were privileged to absorb its beauty.

Living at the farm and sharing it with so many children is something that I will always look back on as a treasured part of my life. I truly loved looking after the kids and was blessed to watch a few trans-formations take place that I don't know would have happened anywhere else.

I can't isolate one single aspect of life on the farm, but when I asked one of the older teens what they thought was the biggest benefit to being in care, their response was profound: "For the first time in my life, I've been allowed to be a child."

11: Don't feed the social workers

Although we were only fostering for a few short years, we still received a cornucopia of children who created a genuine highlight to my life journey. Each and every one of them brought something into our home and left a bit of themselves in my heart when it came time for them to leave. The chronicles they shared and the fortitude and resilience they brandished in working through their own challenges earned them so much respect from me. I'll always be grateful for the lessons they taught me and the opportunity I had to be creative in addressing some complicated behaviours.

I had a lot of fun working with these children and I hope their stay with us gave them something to take away as well.

For us to succeed in providing the best possible experience for foster children in our care, we depended on so many others invested in the same goal. Among the most significant partners we relied on were the two school districts in our area. There were the elementary and high school in Tatamagouche and the junior and senior high school in Truro.

I was involved with teachers' aids, teachers and principals who went above and beyond to give these kids the highest level of care and consideration. Even when some of the children created disruptions in their classes, the staff never altered their commitment to providing exactly what the kids needed.

Our foster home presented a problem for our local schools in that resources are assigned based on the number of students enrolled in September. Because we were the emergency shelter for the entire county, I was often showing up with additional children that the school could not get extra help for. Some of my kids had special needs, and providing the attention they needed was a strain on the schools' already-overburdened system.

Through all this, the kids were never made to feel an inconvenience, and they were always encouraged to participate in everything these schools had to offer. All of these children flourished with the support offered them and it was exciting to watch them discover themselves in ways they'd never experienced before. So much credit is due to our educators for what they do and how they often end up compensating for a lack of support or positive imaging at home.

Social workers are amazing people who can't possibly be paid enough for what they do. They are fewer than they should be, and this is a shortcoming in the resources Social Services has.

I know there is pressure on so many helping agencies, but for some of the kids who came into my care, it had been a long, excruciating road they followed before it was acknowledged that they needed intervention. A lot of time is spent trying to work with families and explore every opportunity to put them on a path to better parenting. The patience of social workers is extensive, but I struggled to emphasize with some parents.

For one child who found their way into our home, Children's Aid had been involved and aides had been coming to their house for a couple of years, giving their mother directions to improve her homemaking skills, like how to roll socks and organize a dresser. The father was a pig who believed any females in the family should be available to the males. With this philosophy, he had done little to discourage his son from torturing and raping two of his sisters for a prolonged period of time. Teaching the mother how to organize a sock drawer wasn't going to make that house a happy home.

It took far too long to get her out of that household. The parents had successfully portrayed their daughter as oppositional and delinquent to anyone who questioned why she kept running away. I know there are protocols that have to be followed, but sometimes wheels turn far too slowly.

Although I found most of the Children's Aid staff to be amazing at what they did, there was one aide I ended up banishing from our property. She was someone who I'm not even sure was a paid employee, but who hung around helping out—possibly as a volunteer? She was the wife of a local clergy member and her being involved with children in care brought her own poisonous perspective to her interactions.

I first met her when she was asked to take a child out to our farm and she seemed quite pleasant at the outset. She complimented our farm and the house and asked if she could have a tour.

I got my daughter to take her around and she did a lot of smiling and nodding, but when we went out to the driveway to say goodbye, our cat Cricket took this occasion to have a seizure.

This was not unusual and he was on medication, but he still experienced the occasional episode where his muscles would stiffen, his head pull back tightly over his back and he would hop around with claws extended as he yowled and hissed.

I'm not sure how I found out, but a social worker probably told me that the church lady had filed a report that my home had satanic overtones and our cat was possessed by a demon. I think Satan was supposed to be living in my daughter's room, where she had on display posters for Nine Inch Nails and The Crow. She was a Goth and also had a few black candles in her room, so this must have set the scene for welcoming evil into our home. The icing on the cake had been our cat hopping and yowling across the driveway as she left.

I didn't bar her yet.

There was another occasion when she was asked to bring one of our regular foster children out after an appointment in town. When the child was dropped off, he told me she had been asking him questions like 'Do we say grace at meals?' and 'Do you say your prayers before you go to bed?' She went so far as to tell this child that he should suggest we do grace and prayers, and I really resented how she tried to manipulate this situation to further her own beliefs. This had absolutely no place in what she was doing.

I still didn't try to restrict her from having contact with our children.

Then the last event was another child being dropped off, this time after we had experienced a blizzard. A large drift blocked the top of the drive-way and my husband had shovelled a path through the snow.

She left her car to trudge down the hill, except she didn't try to come through the break in the drift. Instead, she headed out across country, following the peak of the drift and, from my vantage point, she was getting farther away from us with each step she took, dragging a kid behind her.

I sent my husband out to fetch the child, and at that point I called Children's Aid and told them she was no longer allowed on my property.

I think she was a nickel short of a dollar and I found her religious attitude was toxic towards us. I resented her judgment of our home and the way we conducted ourselves. My daughter and her posters were not a threat to anyone and whether we said grace or not was our business.

Aides and social workers alike were often visitors to the farm and one day, a child was having a regular visit with his worker. I had a large dish of veal scallopini in the oven and the worker commented on how amazing the smell was.

As our meals were always in large quantities, I offered the social worker a seat at the table for supper.

"Oh no!" she said. "You're not allowed to feed social workers."

I thought she was joking. How was it I was restricted from inviting a social worker to sit down to a meal?

Apparently, it had become an issue with social services since some workers were suspiciously timing their visits to coincide with meal times at certain foster homes. They had therefore implemented a policy that no social workers were allowed to accept any invitations to meals.

I found this childish and irritating. Would accepting an invitation lead to preferential treatment? I thought it rude of me if I did not extend the offer of a seat at the table, if the food was available. Would it not have been an opportunity for the social worker to see how their charges interacted in a relaxed, casual setting? I look back on it and still find it silly.

While fostering, we had opportunity to benefit from a lot of training, and both my husband and I volunteered for every workshop or conference available to us. One such conference took place at a distance from our area and carpooling was arranged so as many foster parents as possible could attend.

I was slated to meet up with the parent counsellors who had taken Cynthia into their home and my husband would be dropping me off early in the morning. We would go from her place along with an- other counsellor participant who happened to be the person who had abused Kyle on two occasions.

I was excited and apprehensive at once. I men- tioned on the phone how I looked forward to saying hello to Cynthia while I was at her home and I was immediately shut down. I was requested to not speak to Cynthia, as she would be getting ready for school and could not be interrupted.

This left me speechless. I didn't see the harm in taking a few minutes to speak to her, but they had things tightened down so hard that it would have been a violation of their rules. They asked me to not interfere with everything they had in place and to not make myself known when I was there. They didn't allow her a social life, and why was it so threatening to them that Cynthia have a few minutes to chat?

The day of the conference came and my husband dropped me off as the sun was rising. I was met at the door by the same aloof woman I recalled from a year earlier, when Cynthia had first met her parent counsellor family. She hadn't warmed up any since then.

She asked me to wait in the living room while she finished getting ready and reminded me not to inter- rupt Cynthia as she got ready for school. She didn't even turn the lights on in the living room and, with the curtains still drawn, I was in shadowy darkness and invisible to anyone passing by.

I had mistakenly thought there would be a family

breakfast where they all sat down together, but it couldn't have been farther from reality. I sat quietly, waiting to get going, and eventually Cynthia came quietly up the stairs from her basement room, poured herself a bowl of cereal and took it back downstairs with her. The parent counsellors were in their own room and not a word was exchanged between them.

I wanted to get Cynthia's attention, clear my throat, fake a sniffle, do something! One minute and she was gone. There was no interaction, no good morning, no chatting about the day to come.

The atmosphere was a cold as ice and Cynthia was a prisoner in a home that was vacant of any human connection or intimacy. This was her life and she was subjugated to following their rules. The opposi-tional behaviour would be eradicated by the time they were done and I don't disagree that Cynthia had needed help, but how much of Cynthia would be left when they were done?

The other parent counsellor arrived and we were on our way for a long one-and-a-half-hour drive. I was crammed into the back of a little car and, from the outset, was ostracized from their conversation. I had absolutely nothing in common with either of these women. There wasn't a hope in hell I agreed with their positions of how to discipline a teenager.

Just to frame the one and only topic they dis-cussed during the drive, Cynthia's parent counsellor made the statement, "If you're not making their life miserable, you're doing something wrong!" In this poisonous atmosphere, a young mind was supposed to develop healthy patterns and coping strategies for behavioural issues.

I was so angry to hear her blanket all of her justifications for her own horrible parenting with this rallying cry. Where the hell did Children's Aid find these people?

And the other one in the front seat was still looking after Kyle, even after physically abusing him. How awkward it was to be in the seat behind this monstrosity of nurturing, each of us knowing that I was the safety zone children in her care went to when she was unable to restrain herself.

Children's Aid continued to invite us to become parent counsellors and, knowing what I did, there wasn't a hope I would ever sign up for the program, even if the people involved were caring and sensitive, I just struggled with the intensity of the rules, which resembled those of a military boot camp. My heart ached for both Cynthia and Kyle, and I didn't have a solution for how to fix what was broken.

One thing I did take away from the conference we attended was some advice a guest speaker offered. Not that I was going to follow the advice, but I use it as an example of how out-of-touch some professionals are from the subjects of their focus.

This lady was a psychiatrist from the States with plenty of accolades. She addressed us with a common issue of teens who refuse to clean their room and how we should not get into any heated debates or consequences. Instead, she recommended that we ourselves, clean the room for them, not make a fuss about it and eventually, the teens will feel so guilty about it that they will take over and take responsibility for their own room.

I know of 30-year-old men living at home who still have their room cleaned by their mother.

I wondered how different the kids in the US could be from our teenagers. I am 100% sure that no teenager I've ever met would be so shamed into doing their own room.

I played out a scenario in my mind where a youth, overwhelmed by regret, comes into a room I am cleaning and patting me on the shoulder, tells me it is my job no more. Not in my lifetime.

Workshops were often made available to foster parents and we benefited from the subject and issues they covered. We learned how to be sensitive and supportive of various sexual orientations, with the focus primarily on keeping kids safe. We attended training sessions on how to physically protect ourselves and, if necessary, subdue a child who was out of control and at risk of hurting themselves.

We heard from many wonderful people who shared with us the importance of cultural sensitivity. I remember hearing a lecture from an Indigenous activist, Rita Joe, who talked about growing up in a residential school in our province. These children were so abused and neglected it's understandable they are still trying to come to terms with what happened to them so many years ago.

I bought a book of Rita Joe's poetry, and her words

were not angry. She wanted to be understood and she wanted people everywhere to see who Indigenous people are and how they want to live in today's world, respecting their values and culture.

Along with the educators, teachers and some medical professionals, another group of unsung heroes are foster parents themselves. I am not referring to myself, but to the many others I had the privilege to meet while operating the emergency shelter for our county. There were so many who gave of themselves to create a loving, supportive family environment for both long term and temporary care. Some foster parents end up adopting the children they've been consigned to look after and see these children through to their adulthood.

One family in particular stood out, not because of the strong start they offered children, but because of the dignified end they accorded terminally ill children left in their care. Children's Aid were warriors for so many children who needed their protection, but sometimes special children were introduced to them in very early years, not because parents fell short or were negligent. They just weren't able to deal with the intense medical needs of some kids or the prognosis that they would not see the age of maturity.

It takes special people to cope with a lifelong illness, and this particular foster family was amazing in how they didn't indulge their kids in self-pity. There was just as much structure and discipline exercised over children with special needs as there was over children without extraordinary challenges. They saw their children through frequent visits to hospitals and nights spent sitting beside beds, and were the loving arms that held them when the battles they had with their own bodies left them exhausted and drained.

I met a few of the kids in their care and I confess I would never be able to do what they did. We are lucky to have such people in our world.

Other foster parents had homes that specialized in certain behaviours. There were a couple of families that were trained and highly experienced in working with autistic children. Our home gained a reputation for dealing with behaviourally-challenged teenagers. We were the respite for group homes when they needed a break from their residents on occasion, and for some specialized foster homes who needed a time out from their wards. We were the home of last resort when things weren't working out in other foster homes.

I don't think we did anything that special. I do think kids naturally try to put their best foot forward and, if they were only with me two or three days, it wasn't hard for them to behave. They would soon be back to their regular residence where they could continue to be a terror.

Communities were a big part in supporting foster families. I know there was anxiety from some of our neighbours about what we were doing with so many teens. I think some of them were expecting to see Hell's Angels pull up and destroy the place.

But we had so many friends who welcomed our kids when we visited and, by showing an interest in them, contributed to their confidence and self-esteem. Most children thrive with attention and interest in what they like to do.

I had only one negative experience with another foster parent, which took place during a social event organized by Children's Aid. They approached one of my teen girls, offering to buy her cigarettes for her if she could persuade Children's Aid into switching her over to their care.

I was so disappointed to hear that another foster family would try to pull off such a stunt. They made it very transparent that they were in it for the money, trying to poach children away from their existing families to beef up their own contingent of foster kids. I reported it but never heard the results.

I think one of the surprises I experienced for myself was how much I would genuinely like some of the children's parents. Cynthia's parents were such nice people, very down to earth and not at all hard to get along with. They were out of their element when Cynthia's oppositional behaviour got out of control, but that did not make them bad parents.

Some parents needed to press a 'pause' button while they caught their breath and had an opportunity to become more educated or skilled in dealing with certain behaviours. Even Amanda's mother deserved consideration despite the Fetal Alcohol Syndrome she left with her daughter. What a horror her life had been and judging her, as I initially did, didn't help to save her from herself.

I did, however, find some parents absolute monstrosities and not fit to raise a goldfish. Roberta's mother selfishly put her own social standing ahead of her daughter's right to justice and denied her the protection she deserved from her friend's son. Shane's mother was an evil, manipulative witch who failed parenting at so many levels, using her children to pull of scams, trying to dump her kids on us on Christmas Eve and falsely reporting to Children's Aid that I had allowed Shane access to drugs. She was a real work of art and I thought I heard a rumour that the entire family had been shipped out west.

In years past, I had occasionally heard rumours that when social services had a particularly bothersome client, they sometimes purchased them a bus ticket and sent them off to another province to become somebody else's headache. I wondered if Children's Aid had done the same with Shane's family.

Through our experiences with Children's Aid, I realized they always tried to look at the big picture when taking a child in care. It wasn't just about finding a safer, healthier environment; it was about looking down the road to where this child should be going and how best to get them there. That meant trying to resolve any conflicts at home or offering support to bring the parents to a place where they would be better prepared to deal with the behaviours of their children.

All in all, the social workers, aides, and foster parents worked very hard to set their kids up for success in their futures. If only we lived in a world where they weren't needed! They accomplished wonderful success with so many kids and, although we were only a small part of their journey, we were glad to be there.

We hope all of the kids we met found happiness, and we wish them all the best in what destiny lay ahead. I hope they remember their time with us with affection and fond memories, just as our recollections pay tribute to how special each and every one of them was. Maybe when they grow up, they will open their own homes to children in need, and be inspired by the experience as much as we were.

Kathleen Foster-Alfred

Postscript: Amanda's legacy

Fostering not only affected myself and my husband. It had a lasting impact on my children as well. My daughter Sarah, or Maggie as I refer to her in the book, was particularly affected by Amanda, who was challenged with the effects of Fetal Alcohol Syndrome.

Here are Sarah's thoughts on how knowing Amanda changed her life.

I was seventeen when Amanda first came into my life, and it was my first experience interacting with a person of special needs.

At first, I was incredibly self-conscious and awkward because I was trying my best to not seem in any way condescending towards her. I would eventually learn that it was not part of Amanda's personality to judge me either way. She emulated the feelings of those around her—if you were happy, she was happy, if you were sad, she would be sad, and if you were frustrated, she would be frustrated.

I immediately bonded with her and it was the first time in my life I became aware of a maternal and nurturing instinct, which developed in me in response to her frailties. Amanda taught me so much with her forgiving outlook on the world.

The impact she left with me would carry forward into my future as I decided I wanted to make a difference for the Amandas of the world. I would go on to get a job at a preschool, working with other special needs children, and found out quickly how they would enrich the lives of all of those around them. I then moved worked on school transportation for special needs children in the Halifax Regional Municipality. Throughout my life I have continued to be drawn to challenged children, and not necessarily because I wanted to protect and educate and help them, but also because of how much richer my life has been for having known them.

Amanda is not aware of how she touched my life or how she became a part of me that I carry forward to this day. I believe she will continue to fulfill the needs of others as she goes through life being everything she was ever made to be. She'll never know what she has done for me and, in her typical style, if I'm happy, she's happy.

Sarah (Maggie)

Becoming a foster parent

Anyone considering becoming a foster parent should visit the Nova Scotia Department of Community Services website where, under the sub-title 'Child, Youth and Family Supports', you will find a sub-section: *Programs and Resources - Foster Care*.

The concise introduction they offer is absolutely correct in that you will improve the lives of children in Nova Scotia just by offering yourself, your care, time and attention. These children need the support and love you can bring into their lives, and it will make a difference to someone who needs you.

It is without a doubt one of the most enriching experiences you can bring into your own life, and more people need to check it out. When I look back over the span of my lifetime, nothing compares to the happiness I experienced during those years working with the Foster Care Program in Colchester County. So many amazing children crossed my threshold and I will always be grateful for the opportunity to share a part of their life.

As the Community Services website says,

For more information on becoming a foster

caregiver. call 1-800-565-1884. Or register for a Foster Caregiver Information Session.

Based on feedback received from foster caregivers, children in care and social workers, we're redesigning the foster care program to make sure everyone receives the support they need to thrive.

Help children and youth in your community today. Become a foster caregiver. Be there!

Acknowledgements

I owe many thanks to my family and a friend for their contributions to this book. To my daughter, Sarah Nolan, for her insight and suggestions in bringing this book into the light. To my friend Lynn McLaughlin for some much-appreciated honesty in tightening my focus and offering so many suggestions to enhance my offering.

A special thank-you to Heather Nolan, my daughter-in-law, who's generously offered to take on the task of media manager and handle all aspects of social media. My incompetence in handling anything computer-related is legendary and I have so much faith and appreciation for what she has taken on.

I also want to thank my son, Brent Nolan, and both of my amazing granddaughters, Alex Fraser and Chelsea Nolan. They have always been there to support me and I am blessed to have them in my life.

I struggle to express how much my husband's support means to me. Through so many ideas and brain farts I've had over the years; Wade has never faltered in his encouragement and ability to offer morale support. Throughout our experience fostering, he introduced so many kids to a soft-spoken adult male who didn't abuse anyone or anything. He was able to connect with some kids on a level beyond my ability and kids were able to trust him.

Finally, I wish to thank Andrew Wetmore and Moose House Publications for all their patience and support in making this a dream come true for me. Their immediate trust and acknowledgement of my work has given me the confidence to consider additional writing projects and I can't wait to see what comes next.

About the author

Kay Foster-Alfred grew up in a large military family, familiar with being uprooted and moving to a new home every couple of years. It was a hectic household, where friends were always welcome at the dinner table and lively chatter encouraged. It was natural that she eventually opened her home to children in need of respite and a warm, empathetic heart.

Kay currently lives in Halifax, has two wonderful children and two amazing grand-daughters. She has been active with MADD and the Lions Club in her community and enjoys a quiet life with her husband, Wade.

Kathleen Foster-Alfred

Book group questions

- How important is it that the community accept the ongoing introduction of children passing through their neighbourhood? Should the foster family have had better communications with surrounding residents?
- What pressures might the children and the father of the host family have felt? How might it have changed their lives?
- What, if anything, should have been done when Cynthia was taken to emergency and the doctor appeared apathetic about her emotional state? What should the foster mother have done instead of taking her home?
- Where there other points in the story where, if you were the foster parent, you would have made different choices? How do you think your choices would have worked out?
- Did this foster home offer enough emotional support to meet the needs of their children? How could foster parents be better trained or prepared to deal with some behavioural disorders?
- Should there be privacy for the family to celebrate special occasions that would exclude the

foster children? Would this create some conflict between the biological and foster children?

- Has reading this book encouraged you to become foster parent, or has it caused you to shy away? Why?

- When confronted with an unscheduled meeting with biological parents, how would you suppress the opinion you had formed, based on information Children's Aid gave you? For example, the foster mother did not have a good impression of the baby's biological parents until she was forced to meet them and realized they were just kids themselves.

- Was Rob a victim of a system that failed him or was there something in his early history that set him up for failure? Did his biological parents' abandonment cause psychological trauma that ultimately resulted in his rejection by his adoptive parents?

- Was Cynthia's mother protecting her friends' son by sacrificing her daughter, or was this the result of an age-old, patriarchal attitude toward females bodies?

- Was the punishment of an apology for the theft of a newspaper enough? Was being forced to atone to someone who had an obvious dislike for the foster kids over the top? How would you consequence such an action?

- Do you believe that foster children benefit from the 'It takes a village' ideology that the Children's Aid system creates with professionals such as psychiatrists, psychologists, social workers, teachers and lawyers? What village do/did you have in place when raising your children?

•   How important was it that the home was remote and did not permit the kids easy access to a town or village?

•   Was there any hope for the teen who had learned from an early age to exchange sex for money? How difficult would it be for a foster family create an appealing new life when this child was already patterned to such a damaging lifestyle?

•   Should more programs exist that give the children the positive attention they crave or is that setting them up for disappointment when they mature and that level of focus fades away?

•   Why was it so important to Linda's mother that she share her addiction to cigarettes with her daughter? Did Linda see her spirit wolf because she had lost the protection of her mother and felt vulnerable?

•   In the dispute involving Kevin's teachers aid and the foster mother, should the foster parent have followed the aide's directions for extensive homework, or should Children's Aid have stepped in with clear instructions?

www.ingramcontent.com/pod-product-compliance
Lightning Source LLC
Chambersburg PA
CBHW061146120626
46546CB00005B/1944